Blacks in Nonprofits

Grant Writers Edition

Copyright © 2020 Blacks in Nonprofits

All rights reserved. This book or any portion thereof may not be reproduced or

used in any manner whatsoever without the author's express written permission.

Lisa Nicole Publishing

Lisanicolealexander.com

Gotha, FL 34734

Printed in the United States of America

ISBN: 978-1-7356342-6-5

Dedication

This book is dedicated to black-led nonprofits across the world that give selflessly and pour their heart and soul into their nonprofit each day while trying to find the funding they deserve.

Introduction

This is the first book of its kind- a demonstration of the power of collaboration between experienced African American grant writers. They have decided to come together to provide information, tips, and insider pointers from their experience. This book is packed with opportunities for grant seekers to learn how to design and complete the grant writing process, find funding opportunities, and avoid common pitfalls.

After consulting thousands of nonprofits, I realized the importance of establishing a grant writing book that caters to the African American race in particular. Our funding opportunities and access to resources are not the same. Nonprofits led by people of color are the most underfunded, and I made a personal commitment to begin to change that. Black-led nonprofits receive less than 4% of grants and contributions each year. We have formed an amazing community of Blacks in Nonprofits with over 17,000 black-led nonprofits and black business owners who provide a service to them.

This book is the first of many resources that people of color will have that focuses on the struggles and hurdles they go through to receive funding. It is time to shed light on these issues to create much needed social change. Our amazing grant experts reveal the secrets that make grants compelling to funders, the red flags you should avoid, and how to create relationships with funders. Each expert shares their personal experiences and lessons learned throughout their years of experience in the nonprofit sector.

Many people that will read this book have goals to pursue a career as a grant writer, and with the help of the amazing grant writers that contributed their journeys in the book, there are tons of lessons to learn from. It is our hope that we continue to change the narrative of African Americans in the nonprofit sector and continue to provide resources, tools, and the support needed to run their nonprofits successfully. We are leaving a legacy for the next generations to come and provided hope to black-led nonprofits all over the world.

Dr. Rho
President
National Nonprofit Minority Association

Table of Contents:

Regeanie S. Corona

Website: www.regeanie.com

Facebook: https://www.facebook.com/regeanie

Instagram: https://www.instagram.com/regeanie

LinkedIn: https://www.linkedin.com/in/regeaniecorona/

Regeanie is a business development strategist, nonprofit specialist, author, speaker, trainer, and purpose life coach with over 30 years of experience in Information Technology, Business Systems Development, and Integration, Business Development, Strategic Planning, and training/development.

She has worked in both the public and private sectors. She has managed multimillion-dollar projects and has helped raise over $6.5M in support of community development, economic development, and public health-related projects benefiting underserved individuals. Driven by a desire to help others thrive in life and business, she now assists current and aspiring nonprofit leaders and social entrepreneurs in achieving maximum efficiency in running and growing their operations.

With more than 17 years of leadership experience, she has also learned to utilize her skills to help organizations from multiple sectors come together in collaborative partnerships to build strong and healthy communities.

She is the Founder and CEO of Advancing the Seed Inc., a 501(c)3 nonprofit organization based in Southern California whose mission is to develop strong business and community engagement leaders.

I am a business strategist, nonprofit expert, purpose and goal-setting life coach, trainer, speaker, and author. I grew up in Compton, California, with amazing parents who provided a solid home life filled with lots of love. My mom was responsible for giving me a strong faith in Jesus Christ, and my dad role-modeled entrepreneurship and chasing your dreams. They both instilled in me a strong work ethic. As a middle schooler, I discovered a love for writing. I wanted to write every chance that I got. As I moved into high school, this love for writing continued. I would write short stories and poetry, and I discovered that anything given as a school writing assignment generally came with ease.

Eventually, as I moved into a professional setting in adulthood, I enjoyed writing training manuals, presentations, proposals, business memos, and the like. It was as though I gained energy from the writing process. This brings us to today in 2020. I continue to thoroughly enjoy the process of writing, and I am continuing to learn tricks, hacks, and techniques to help me become a better writer every day.

Grant writing was not an intentional decision on my part. It became a means to an end. I wanted to help nonprofits find funding, and I loved writing, so I took a desire to serve and combined it with that love and found a way to have a greater impact in the marketplace. It was an intersection between passion, purpose, and a business idea.

In 2013, just after leaving a long career in local government as a senior manager in the Information Technology and Cybersecurity field, I served as a volunteer with an organization doing really great work with women going through substance abuse recovery. Like other grassroots and startup organizations, they had an amazing mission but desperately needed funding to impact more individuals. I was familiar with grants and proposal evaluation, as well as writing large-scale work plans for multimillion-dollar projects. I quickly decided that seeking money for a small organization couldn't be too much different than for a larger one, just on a much smaller scale. I dove in with everything that I had, and I've never looked back!

Since 2014, I have personally written and helped guide others to write grant proposals and letters of inquiry (LOI) that have resulted in awards totaling more than 7.2 million dollars.

This doesn't include the grant proposals that I have written that resulted in thousands of dollars of pro-bono services and donated products. I am grateful that I have a record of about 70 percent of all grants applied for being awarded. I attribute this mostly to the fact that I am extremely selective in the types of grants that I go after, whether it is for a client or my own organization.

I am a firm believer that organizations should never desperately "chase" money, applying for funding dollars that don't align with their mission, vision, values, or core programs. This is a big mistake that can lead to shifting priorities and unsustainability. According to GuideStar by Candid, one of the best things you can do in grant writing is to "tie the program to the funder's interests."

When organizations try to adjust their programs to "fit" the funder's priorities, it is usually a wasted effort. Other organizations whose programs do properly align with the funder are also submitting proposals and are likely to be considered above your submission. Be sure that you are increasing your chances of the award by only going after the opportunities that are the strongest fit for your organization's programs/projects.

I also attribute my successful grant outcomes to learning about the Community Reinvestment Act in the financial world and Corporate Social Responsibility in the general corporate world. While I have successfully applied for many foundation grants and some government grants, I decided to focus most of my grant writing efforts on these two specific areas of grant-seeking.

In most cases, this has allowed me to identify the grants that I will have the highest likelihood of winning. This is based on the proper alignment of the funder's priorities to those of my organization or my client's organization and developing the right relationships to bring those grant opportunities to my attention.

Very much like finding a niche in business so that you can hone your skills and narrow your focus to allow you to increase your desired outcomes, many grant writers have discovered niche areas of focus that they can thrive in. For some, it is based on the industry; for others, it is based on grant type (such as government or foundation grants). I have found that my greatest success has come in seeking grants that are provided by banks and corporate funders for small nonprofits who are doing good work in their communities by addressing some of the most disparate needs.

While I no longer take on new clients, I love teaching and coaching leaders of small or startup nonprofits (those with annual revenues of less than $100,000). I love teaching them the strategies needed to create sustainable revenue with consistent monthly cash flow and how to utilize CRA and CSR funding sources.

The first grant proposal that I ever wrote was in the form of a Letter of Inquiry (LOI) for $2,700 to support an annual event for women recovering from substance abuse. I had never written an LOI, but I had written business proposals that resulted in thousands of dollars of business funding. I assumed this would be similar. After successfully obtaining this first small grant, I wanted to learn all that I could about the grant writing process. I took numerous classes, read many books, and asked others in the nonprofit space for guidance.

Initially, it appeared that the grant writing process was complex. Then, through colleagues and mentors, I became aware of and participated in a University of Southern California (USC) certificate program designed to help equip local minority faith leaders with the knowledge and resources to successfully seek funding for their nonprofits and churches from the corporate world.

The Faith Leaders' Institute (FLI) was a program of the Cecil Murray Center for Community Engagement under the tutelage of Reverend Dr. Cecil Murray and Reverend Dr. Mark Whitlock.

They served as great mentors teaching myself and others how to develop programs to address our respective communities' needs and how to seek partners in the banking and corporate communities to help address those needs through funding and volunteerism. In case you are unfamiliar with these two leaders in the African American faith community, Rev. Murray led the rebuilding of South Los Angeles after the 1992 riots. Rev. Whitlock, who is now senior pastor of Reid Temple AME Church in Glenn Dale, Maryland, worked closely with him and led First AME Church's FAME Renaissance economic development program.

Rev. Murray and Rev. Whitlock's work brought jobs, housing, and $400 million in corporate investment to the South Los Angeles community at a time when it was desperately needed. Rev. Whitlock had a background working in commercial real estate. He had also served as an executive at Wells Fargo Bank and Chicago Title Insurance Co.

With Rev. Murray's spiritual leadership in the community and Rev. Whitlock's shrewd knowledge of business and investments, the two men paved the path for more leaders of color in Southern California to repeat these outcomes in their community and economic development efforts. I am grateful to have been mentored by these two results-driven leaders and to be able to say that I am a successful product of their teaching and coaching.

During the FLI program, I learned the intricacies of seeking grant funding with banks and corporate partners, as well as how to articulate the problem statement and support it with the necessary data that clearly demonstrated the problem. I learned the value of storytelling to connect funders to the emotional side of the issues.

The funding strategies that were taught during the program also emphasized understanding the Community Reinvestment Act (CRA) and Corporate Social Responsibility (CSR), primarily because these were strategies that were successfully leveraged by Rev. Murray and Rev. Whitlock in their efforts to rebuild South Los Angeles after the 1992 riots.

This has been invaluable information and has served my grant-seeking efforts well. This is also one of the areas that I have spent most of my time advocating in, learning about, and seeking funding partnerships because I have had very positive results. I have built phenomenal relationships and have learned more than I ever imagined about bank community giving programs.

The first opportunity that I had to utilize my newly discovered knowledge was in a grant proposal and pitch-meeting with a local bank in 2014. The grant amount was $10,000, and I submitted the request on behalf of an organization where I was a board member and provided volunteer operational support. This was also the first real opportunity to put the strategies that I learned from the FLI program into action.

What is CRA?

The Community Reinvestment Act was signed into law in 1977 by President Jimmy Carter. Its purpose was to encourage banks and thrift institutions to "serve the convenience and needs of the communities in which they are chartered to do business," including low- and moderate-income (LMI) communities.

According to Federal Reserve History (federalreservehistory.org), the CRA requires that each federal bank regulator evaluate the extent to which banks address the credit needs of LMI neighborhoods in their geographic markets. Prior to the passing of the CRA, banks were notorious for not marketing their lending products and financial services to LMI communities. This was a practice known as "redlining."

It was another way of suppressing wealth-building for LMI communities by restricting access to mortgage and business lending products. Redlining was part of discriminatory lending practices and was illegal. The final CRA bill directed the federal regulatory agencies to assess the institution's record of meeting the credit needs of its entire community, including LMI neighborhoods, and to take this record into consideration when the banking institution is being evaluated for mergers and acquisitions.

The CRA also allowed for the Federal Reserve Board's Community Development function. This function was created to help community groups navigate the process of protesting against a bank if they felt their practices were discriminatory. It was referred to as Community Affairs.

The Federal Reserve Board then asked each of the Reserve Banks to set up a similar group. Community groups became much more skilled at navigating the protest process on their own. In doing so, they began seeking relationships with banks to address their concerns and propose opportunities to fund community programs and projects.

Simultaneously, since banks were looking for community investment opportunities, they began looking for stronger relationships with community groups. As a result, the original community affairs role moved to become one of coordinating relationship-building to addressing economic challenges and hardships in LMI communities. (It is important to note that credit unions do not fall under CRA rules, but many are just as interested in partnering with local community organizations to be an active part of investing in the needs of the communities that they operate in and serve.)

When banks contribute funds, services, or products to a nonprofit organization, they receive CRA credits, which in turn contributes to their overall CRA rating.

This rating is important to many banks, especially the larger ones, because (among other things) it is used to help determine whether a bank is allowed to successfully participate in acquisitions and mergers. I am vastly oversimplifying the concept. Mostly because my primary point is not to give you the intricate details of how CRA processes work in a banking institution, but to help you understand what it is, why it is important to banks, and how to leverage it to create partnerships that will help you carry out your social mission.

Banks need community partners to help meet their CRA goals because they don't have widespread, direct access to the community they wish to serve, and nonprofits need banking partners to help support their work. It is a very healthy symbiotic relationship. There are some who believe that CRA is no longer necessary. However, for many community organizations in LMI communities, it is a pathway to funding, pro bono services, and volunteerism that is critical to helping meet the needs of those they serve. It is important that small community organizations develop relationships with local banks in their communities.

Most banks have an identified CRA manager who is responsible for managing the CRA activities for their bank. This is a great person to connect with and ask about the different community investments that the bank has established as priorities. Many CRA managers participate in local community events and are very approachable. It would also be beneficial to become familiar with the Federal Reserve Bank responsible for your local area and seek out information about what they are involved in to support LMI community efforts.

While many banks focus a larger percentage of their CRA funds on lending, housing, and economic and community development, they also dedicate a significant percentage of funding for ancillary activities that support major categories such as financial literacy, homebuyers' education, small business training, and technical assistance. They also dedicate a percentage of funds to support local human services and humanitarian activities. As you research the banks in your area, you can generally find information online about their specific areas of giving and where they place the highest priorities for giving.

It is also important to know that local bank branches often have a smaller giving budget and can choose to invest in programs and projects that the branch manager feels is a good fit for the bank's giving priorities. These amounts are usually much smaller but can be a great way to build a relationship with the bank and get the local support needed to apply for a larger amount later through the bank's larger CRA-based giving program. These local relationships can also be important in obtaining volunteers and board members.

For example, if you do a Google search for "Bank of America community giving," you will likely get a search result that lists something along the lines of "Bank of America community grants & general operating support." Clicking this link will take you to Bank of America's page that provides information on how to find grants and sponsorships offered by their bank. From there, you can learn the details of their various giving programs, contact information if available, and a link to apply for funding. Understanding how to do simple research to uncover funding opportunities is an important tool to add to your toolbox when you are a startup or small organization that may not have the resources to hire a grant writer.

Besides gathering details about the bank's community giving program, you should search for news or current events about the bank. Specifically, search for mergers, acquisitions, or even public relations issues that they may be dealing with (especially if it relates to disenfranchisement or unsatisfactory support of low-to-moderate income communities or minority groups).

Why? Because these are the times that banks are usually more eager to perform community outreach as a part of their public relations efforts. It is always important to understand where the business benefits exist for both sides of the relationship and highlight those benefits when pitching your program or project for funding opportunities.

In addition to the research that you perform on the bank itself, leverage online professional networking tools, such as LinkedIn (www.linkedin.com) and Alignable (www.alignable.com), to search your network for connections to individuals that can help you obtain an introduction to CRA officers and staff. This can go a long way to reducing the amount of time that it takes to develop an initial relationship compared to a cold call or email.

In 2017 and 2018, I had the opportunity to be part of a group that traveled to our nation's capital to advocate for continued CRA support and investments in LMI communities.

During this time, I was fortunate to sit in meetings with individuals such as the previous Comptroller of the Currency, Joseph Otting, the Secretary of the Treasury, Steven Mnuchin, the Board of Governors and Federal Reserve Bank leaders, and Chairman of the Federal Reserve, Jerome Powell.

Regardless of what anyone's political views are or what you think of any given administration, it is important to be part of critical conversations that can determine the fate of funding dollars and support in your local area. Early in my career, I was told that "you are either at the table and part of the conversation, or you are being served to those at the table." I've always chosen to be at the table rather than being "served up" to those at the table. This means that others are making decisions that impact you, and you didn't weigh in on the decision. I hope that I can encourage each of you reading this chapter to be involved, be active, and be part of the group sitting at the table and engaging in the critical conversations that are helping to drive decisions that impact you and those you serve.

What is CSR?

Corporate Social Responsibility is a self-regulating business model that is practiced by companies of all sizes. It is a concept that allows businesses to take an active role in being accountable for their actions to both their stakeholders and the public. When corporations outline clear social responsibility strategies, they demonstrate a commitment to be responsible and accountable for their economic, social, and environmental impact on society.

Today, many large and mid-sized companies have social responsibility strategies and goals in place, ranging from corporate giving programs to volunteering programs that encourage employees to volunteer with local charities. Job seekers and consumers are much more inclined to seek out a company to work for or do business with that is socially conscious. Similar to the way that banks execute CRA activities, many companies have formal community giving programs.

In addition to budgets that are designated for giving grants to nonprofits whose programs and projects align with the company's giving priorities, many corporate giving programs incorporate pro bono services.

These products can include free software licenses, product discounts, employee contribution match programs, and employee volunteer support.

Many of the companies with CSR strategies in place need local community nonprofits to meet their annual goals. Often, the nonprofit serves as the bridge to reach the audiences of people that the corporation simply cannot. Similar to my work in the financial world, I have been fortunate to sit in meetings with CEO's and key leaders for companies such as Charter Communications, Frontier, Verizon, Lyft, Uber, and others.

Building these key relationships has allowed me to seek funding support and sponsorship for my organization and clients that I might not otherwise have been able to do easily. I can't stress enough the importance of being in the room and participating in these key conversations if you have the opportunity to do so. Sometimes it requires that you join associations or coalitions that are working toward common goals so that you can have access to these resources; it can definitely be worth the investment of your time and money for any membership fee that is required.

Organizations like the National Nonprofit Minority Association (www.nationalnonprofitminorityassociation.org) can provide a great avenue for you to make these vital connections. Additionally, like with the financial institutions, it is wise to seek out the community giving program managers and try to develop a meaningful relationship to learn more about their giving and how you can potentially partner with them (if it is a right fit).

You can follow many of the same research tactics that I identified earlier when searching for community giving programs from companies that have CSR practices embedded in their business model. With CSR programs, you might not initially get access to cash funding, but you could get access to products, pro bono services, or volunteers like with banks. These options can be like cash to your budget, so please don't discount them.

For example, if a large legal firm takes on your organization as a pro bono client, you could receive thousands of dollars in services at no cost to your organization. This is invaluable. One awesome CSR benefit to nonprofits is access to free or discounted software.

Some of these products can be accessed via membership with TechSoup (www.techsoup.org), a nonprofit providing access to negotiated technology and software deals to other nonprofits. Many technology companies will provide direct access to discounts or even free access to their products.

If you are considering purchasing a software product, ALWAYS reach out to the company and ask if they offer discounts to nonprofits. My experience is that 95% of them do, but it is not always advertised or common knowledge. I have saved my organization and my clients thousands of dollars on software alone.

Since I come from a technology background, I am very process-driven. I learned quickly that I could overcome many grant-writing hurdles by simply creating processes that I could easily repeat each time I had a new grant to apply for. Below, I am sharing my top 10 strategies and processes that have led to a high yield of return on grant awards.

Strategies for Small or Startup Organizations Seeking CRA or CSR Grant Opportunities

1. **Create a digital footprint** – Make sure that you have a web presence so that others can research your organization and the work that it is doing. Try performing a Google search on your organization. The results will give a clear indication as to what a potential funder will find about the work that you are doing on an initial search. Consider maintaining a Facebook Business Page and a landing page connected to an internet domain (URL). Many organizations will find that they don't need a fully developed website. A single landing page with a continuous scroll that can clearly state your mission and vision, core values, who you serve, outcomes and testimonials, your leadership, your partners and/or funders, a donate button, and a place to accept email opt-ins are a great start to legitimizing your organization's work from a public research perspective. Additionally, consider creating an account and filling out an organization profile on GuideStar by Candid. Many funders, potential individual donors, and others will look up your organization on GuideStar before they consider donating or

volunteering to provide support. This is probably more important than ever as we shift the way we do business to a more virtual environment.

2. **Research local banks and corporations** – Look at the banks and corporations in your local community. Create a list of the top 10 to 15. Do a Google search for each entity on your list by searching for the entity name plus the phrase "community giving program." This should return information about their giving program, hopefully providing a web page with more detailed information. You will want to pay special attention to (1) giving priorities, (2) grant opportunities, (3) requirements for grant opportunities, (4) grant cycle or submission deadlines, (5) all types of giving (not just cash grants), (6) list of prior grant awardees (and amounts if available), and (7) who to contact. Most banks and corporations will list this information on a company web page or direct you to their corporate foundation website (if they have one). If you have access to a grants database, look up the entity in the database and search for more detailed information, such as their past giving, the

organizations that they gave to, and the amounts given. If they have a separate foundation to handle their community giving, you should be able to search for and find this information on their foundation's 990 tax return. This information is important because it will allow you to see if they have given support to organizations that are similar to yours and how much was given. Lastly, if you can contact them, do so. A phone call to the program manager or CRA officer is best to establish a relationship. Tell them about your organization and the work that you do. Let them know that you have a program or project that you believe aligns well with their priorities and you would like to find out how to establish a relationship with them so that you can be considered for a funding opportunity.

3. <u>Develop key relationships</u> - The best way to create relationships is to connect with people on a genuine level, either in person or virtually. Leverage social media and professional associations to reach out and ask for a meeting. The worst thing that could happen is the person says no or doesn't respond. Since we are experiencing unique times due

to the COVID-19 pandemic, in-person events are not occurring frequently, or even at all in many cases. Attending events where you know that some of the key individuals that you wish to meet would have been one of the best ways to make connections and develop relationships. However, while social distancing remains prevalent, you will have to be more creative in making these connections. Many entities are replacing in-person events with virtual ones, and they are using cloud-based software and mobile apps that allow people to network and set up virtual meetings. I encourage you to consider this as a viable option and approach it with the same strategies and goals that you would have an in-person event. When in-person events become common again, I suggest that you quickly resume relationship-building and networking. Please remember that as you build these relationships, don't expect to have immediate funding results from many of them. While funders understand that non-profits are looking to connect with them, they are also approached by so many non-profit's that they can't be responsive to them all. Sometimes you have to be patient and take time to nurture a relationship and explore the possibilities so that you don't appear desperate for funding.

4. Pitch a low-risk project to establish partner relationships. Sometimes the best way to open the path to a funding relationship is to pitch a low-risk project that will allow the funder to "test" the relationship before they go all in. This is especially true if you are a start-up organization and have been operating for less than 12 months and haven't yet built a solid funding strategy that generates consistent revenue. A funder never wants to be the sole funder of a program or project. They feel much more confident in making an investment when they can see that other funders are coming to the table with part of the investment as well. Keeping this in mind, it might be extremely difficult to get a funder to give you $15,000 for a program if you haven't secured any other funding. However, if you have a smaller-scale version of your program that you could treat as a pilot and ask the funder to support it with a small investment to test out viability, they may be willing to take the risk. Be sure to clearly lay out the project objectives

and goals, expected outcomes, and what you will measure as success. Additionally, indicate how the project will help them accomplish their goals. Remember, while they may want to help support your efforts, it still needs to be a good business decision. Help them see "what's in it for them" and how it will be mutually beneficial.

5. <u>Create boilerplate documents</u> – Some entities will have a formalized grant submission process, and others will ask for a Letter of Inquiry (LOI) and a simple budget. The less formalized the process, generally, the easier and faster it is to obtain funding. In some cases, you may only need to meet with someone to pitch the idea, provide a one-page description (including project amount), and an invoice for payment. These are the best types of grant opportunities. Regardless, it pays to be prepared to respond quickly. I always recommend that my clients develop boilerplate documents. This is essentially a document that follows a proposal structure and contains information about your organization, the problem you are solving, how you are solving it, and all other

relevant details. I suggest creating an overall organizational boilerplate, which contains the background details for your organization and all information that is generally related to your organization. I then suggest having boilerplate documents for each of your major programs outlining the problem that the program addresses, how you solve the problem, who you are solving it for, the program methodology, program goals and objectives, a process for measurement and evaluation, the anticipated outcomes and impact, and a program budget with a narrative. Depending on your specific structure, update the program boilerplate to reflect the budget and any other details that require updating at the end of each calendar or fiscal year. These boilerplate documents will become the basis for your grant and LOI submissions in the upcoming year. You can also give them out to board members, volunteers, outsourced grant writers, or anyone else who may assist you in your grant writing efforts. You will be able to use "snippets" from these documents to complete 70% of the grant applications that you go after. You will likely be able to pull from these documents to generate LOIs and pitches as well. Be sure to store the files in a cloud-based centralized file management repository such as Google Drive or Dropbox so that you can easily share with others on your team who will need access to them.

6. <u>Focus on outcomes and impact</u> – When you present your program or project to a funder, clearly identify the problem that you are solving, and then place great emphasis on the outcomes that you will achieve and how those outcomes will result in impact. Some non-profit leaders confuse outputs and outcomes, and while both are important, today's funders are looking for outcomes that lead to change and lasting impact. To clarify, the output is an action that your organization does and can generally be counted. An outcome defines changes that have occurred because of the action. For example, if your organization has a youth program and teaches 11 to 15-year olds how to write computer code two hours per week for ten weeks, that is the action. However, the desired outcomes are to increase interest in STEM-related careers, reduce time spent after school in at-risk behavior, and improve critical thinking and problem-solving. Quantitative and qualitative

indicators can measure these outcomes over a period of time to validate the theory of change. It is important to clearly articulate that the funder's investment will do more than simply result in "boxes checked" or quantities met. It is worth noting that an exception to this rule would be if the funder is simply looking for outputs. In that case, it is perfectly fine to indicate anticipated outputs if that meets the funder's requirements (this is highly unusual in current funding communities). For example, if the funder is only interested in the number of meals that you provide to homeless individuals and not looking for you to reduce the number of homeless individuals in the community, then your outcomes would be more tactical and speak to ensuring that the homeless receive at least one hot, nutritious meal per day from your program.

7. <u>Create a grants support repository</u> – One of the most important processes that I learned and implemented early in my grant writing career was to create a centralized repository of grant assets for myself and my clients. I generally create a folder called "Grants." Within that folder, I create a subfolder

called "General Support Docs." Inside of this subfolder, I store the IRS 501(c)3 determination letter, a current list of board members and officers with their affiliations, a current list of funders and the amount of funding by program/project, the Conflict of Interest policy, board agreement and give/get policy, letters of support, and copies of the last two 990EZ (if available). I also create another subfolder under the "Grants" folder called "Marketing Materials." In this subfolder, I store copies of brochures, testimonials, pictures, and other marketing information about the organization and its accomplishments. My experience is that there is a lot of valuable time lost searching for documents are required for grant submissions and pitch presentations. When these documents that are needed repeatedly are stored in a common location, it cuts down considerably on the amount of time spent searching for them each time they are needed.

8. <u>Present a logical and structured case for support</u> – First, structure your LOI or grant proposal according to the funder's requirements. Then, structure it according to a standard

proposal structure. There should be a clear flow from one aspect of the proposal narrative to the other. Most proposals start with a statement of the problem and then flow into how your organization meets that problem. If the funder provides a list of questions to answer in the proposal, be sure to structure those questions in an organized and structured manner so that proposal evaluators will not have to struggle to understand your overall proposal response.

9. **Be willing to accept pro bono services, product donations, and/or volunteers initially instead of cash.** Most times, as a start-up or smaller organization, especially if you have not acquired grant funding yet, it can be a bit more challenging to get a cash donation. I've already shared one way to address this problem in strategy #4. Another strategy is to approach a potential funding partner with an ask for pro bono services, product donations, and/or volunteers. It is important to remember that these items have a cash value, and while you might not have cash in hand when you receive one of them, it results in cash savings. If you paid someone to perform the

service or do the work, or if you purchased the product(s), it would be an expense from your budget. In this case, you won't have to incur the cost because the funding partner is providing it. In some cases, this can be more important than a cash grant, especially if the amount of money that it saves your organization is significant. Sometimes it is easier for a potential funding partner to establish a relationship through one of these activities versus writing a check. As the relationship grows and the funder learns more about your organization, the work you do, and your ability to deliver on your stated outcomes, they are more inclined to provide greater commitment and support, including a cash donation.

10. **Ask for the right amount of money** – So many organization leaders are disappointed when they hear the dreaded "no" in response to a grant application submission or a LOI request. While many factors go into the grant award process, one big mistake that start-up or small non-profit leaders make is to ask for an amount that is disproportionate to the amount of their budget. Many of us have experienced the desperate need to

increase our revenue to carry forth our mission and have heard that grant money or "free money" is the best way to fund our efforts. While grants are very necessary to your organization's sustainability, for most non-profit's, regardless of size, grant revenue accounts for about 33% of the overall revenue strategy. When looking at grants from CRA or CSR sources, a general rule that I apply is to ask for approximately 10-15% of your overall budget. Of course, there are exceptions to this rule, but it tends to stand in many cases. One exception to the rule might be if you have a contact who works with the funding entity, and they have instructed you to apply for more. I will warn that even if someone on the "inside" has recommended that you ask for more, be certain that they are familiar with the entity's formal review process and your organization's specific budget details because a misguided recommendation could still result in your request being denied. In some cases, the funder will evaluate the amount you've asked for and will award you BUT will automatically decrease the amount that they award based on the budget information you've submitted. In other cases, the funder will reject your request altogether because you've asked for an amount that doesn't proportionately align with your budget, and it becomes a red flag to the reviewers that you don't really understand your budget or the grant request process. My general recommendation is to practice asking for no more than 10-15% of your overall organizational or program budget (depending on the type of funding that you are asking for) because this often increases your chances of receiving a "yes," especially since you are only asking the funder to bear a fraction of the overall revenue needed to support your request. As with other things, this is not a hard and fast rule, and you may find that you have more flexibility in the asking amount, depending on the scenario. However, if you are just beginning to build your budget, you might have greater success in the first 12-18 months, asking multiple funders for smaller amounts versus going after larger amounts that seem unrealistic for your size, capacity, and existing budget. As I stated before, there are exceptions to this rule, and if you have the ability to leverage a relationship that can help you obtain funding that is a much larger percentage of your budget, then by all means, go for it.

Grant seeking does not have to be complicated. It is definitely an activity that requires time, focus, and consistent hard work, but it isn't out of your reach. I recommend that you take time with your board in the early part of the 4th quarter of each year to develop your revenue strategy for the following year. This includes developing your new budget and outlining the sources that will make up your revenue streams. This should include a healthy mix of donations, grants, sponsorships, and earned income.

As you build your grants portfolio and your overall income, look at banking and corporate partners that you personally like and support. See if their brands align with the mission and values of your organization. Sometimes these funding opportunities can be simpler to achieve and will give you the needed experience to go from receiving smaller amounts to much larger amounts. Before you know it, you will find yourself with a steady influx of revenue, allowing you to have positive month-to-month cash flow and financial sustainability much sooner than you think. And remember, relationships are key to successful fundraising.

Annette J. Morris, M.A

Facebook: Goal Getter LLC

Instagram: Goal_Getter_University

Website: www.goalgetterforever.com

Email: goalgetterllc@gmail.com

Annette J. Morris, M.A., is a professional Mental Health Counselor, Certified Life Coach, motivational speaker, published author, entrepreneur, and business consultant. Her favorite quote, which is the philosophy she lives by, is "you will get all you want in life if you help enough people get what they want" by the late Zig Ziglar. Her professional career is focused solely on helping others to either accomplish their goals as an entrepreneur or in life as a whole. Although Annette has accomplished a lot in life, she had very humble beginnings. She was reared for 23 years in a local housing project by a single mother and had to overcome many obstacles on this journey called life. However, all that she's endured in her past has helped to form the Annette of the present. Annette is a first-generation college graduate and has earned a Bachelor of Arts in Psychology from Southern University of New Orleans and a Master of Arts from Xavier University of Louisiana. She's also the first full-time entrepreneur of her family and Owner/Lead Consultant of Goal Getter, LLC. Annette has also published three books: Conquering the EneME; Live Free: Creating the Streams to Live Your Dreams; Everyday's a New Day: Daily Positive Affirmations for Positive Daily Living and Streams Reloaded: The Entrepreneur's Guide to Multiple

Streams of Income. She also co-authored a project entitled I Want to

Quit My Job: 8 Entrepreneurial Tips for Massive Results While

Employed. She's also spearheaded a co-author project entitled Favor

in Failure. Of all that she's accomplished in life, she's most excited

about being saved and a child of the most high God.

Foundation Grants and Grant Readiness

I can remember when I started my first nonprofit organization 12 years ago. I had a desire to teach kids the skills they needed but weren't being taught in school, mainly life and social skills. I realized the kids I was working with as a therapist lacked the basic skills to establish and maintain relationships, conflict resolution, anger management, and the list goes on. So, as a therapist, I'd assure the deficiency in these skills were addressed in their treatment plan. However, it led me to wonder how many other kids lacked these skills. My research caused me to determine that these skills are not taught in schools, so I went on a crusade to "help the kids."

In my mind, because I'm a skilled, trained professional, "save the people person" became my drive and mission. I started a nonprofit organization; the focus was on teaching life and social skills to youth and adolescents. We partnered with a few schools on a contractual basis to teach our curriculum. However, I desired to do more. At the time, I was employed full time as well as running the organization.

Therefore, when we needed something that exceeded the minimal funding we were generating from the contract work, I'd just pay for it out of pocket. Fortunately for me, I had a Vice President that was also an MBA. One day at a Board meeting, she said, in a nutshell, she understood my ambition to help people, but we need money. I'm thinking *God will provide*. She's said, "yep, he will--as soon as we get a plan to generate money." She was raining on my parade, of course, but she was right. There was no way we could do all that the mission required us to do without revenue.

This led me to fall back on a skill that I'd learned in graduate school, grant writing. I thought, like most nonprofit Directors, we need grants to get this thing going. I started researching grants in the first place I'd heard of (grants.gov). When you're new to the grant writing space, grants.gov is the last place you want to visit because the site can be overwhelming. There are tons of grants there, but they're state and federal grants. New to the grant writing space, these types of grants are very detailed and require a lot. Federal grants are definitely not for newbies. The more research I conducted, the more I realized all hope was not lost.

There are other options aside from federal grants. I stumbled across a directory that housed Foundation Grants. Although the directory housed (I believe) every foundation known to man, it was half as overwhelming as grants.gov. I began clicking on options one by one to see that the RFP's were less demanding and easier to respond to than those of federal grants. For me, foundation grants have been the way to go. I'm sure you're now asking what foundation grants are and how do you find them. Well, let's talk about them.

Foundation Grants

Foundation grants are one of the primary sources for grants, especially for nonprofit organizations. Most foundations are funded by the corporations they're connected to or by endowments from a single individual or group of individuals. For example, Walmart has a foundation, Target has a foundation, Kellogg's---yes, the cereal people--also have a foundation. As you can see, these foundations are attached to the corporations.

However, you will also have foundations that are funded by individuals like Bill and Melinda Gates and Edward Wisner; Wisner was a philanthropist that died and left 100 years of funding for organizations that services youth, community development, and beautification for organizations doing great works in the City of New Orleans.

When attempting to understand the difference in Foundation grants and Federal grants, just know:

- Government grants, although their ceiling (the maximum amount of funding they will give in funding for the term of the grant) and floor (the least amount they will give in funding for the term of the grant) rewards will exceed that of a foundation grant, are very labor-intensive. Most organizations that apply for federal grants have a team dedicated to compiling the grant for this very reason.

- Foundation grants, although possessing smaller monetary value, are easier to apply for than federal grants. They are also a lot less time consuming to compile.

- Most payments are in advance (once a grant is approved). This is different from federal grants, in which many are reimbursement grants. This means your organization will have to have the funding necessary to jump-start the program and bill the government for reimbursement (in increments). If you're awarded $500,000, please understand you will not be granted the entire balance upfront, but in increments, as you provide programming in alignment with what was stated in your grant submission.

I encourage those that are new to the grant writing space to start with foundation grants because they are less demanding to write and can be completed in one sitting by an individual. When you're able to secure foundation grants, it will enhance the self-esteem of the writer to make the decision to move into the high demanding space of federal grant writing.

Types of Foundation Grants

Some of the most common types of grants are:

In-Kind Grants-These are grants that are not monetary. However, they have a monetary value. Some entities will provide services to nonprofit organizations at no cost to the organization. The service must be in alignment with the provider and the organization's mission. For example, if the organization provided youth enrichment services, a dance school may volunteer 25 hours of services. Typically, they would charge $50.00 per hour. However, as an in-kind donation, they're giving the hours to the nonprofit free of charge. It's still valued at $50.00 an hour; therefore, the in-kind granted amount is $1,250.00.

Program grants-These funders allocated their funding to support specific programs or projects for a pre-determined period. For example, the Kellogg Foundation has provided grant funding to organizations for a 3-year period. This means after three years, the entity should have found another means to replace that particular funding.

Operating fund grants- These grants provide ongoing support to an organization helping with operating expenses. Small, family foundations are more likely to provide operating fund grants than larger, well-known foundations.

Locating Foundation Grants

Many are unsure of where to locate foundation grants to assist with funding their organizations. In conducting grant research, it's more than just finding an organization giving away money. There's no shortage of funding in the land, so it's not pressing that you attempt to squeeze into any organization's funding pool. If you are an organization servicing the elderly and the funder is funding boys' programs, don't run out and create a boy's program. Instead, move to the next organization.

In conducting grant research, you want to start by finding organizations that align with your mission. There will be many funders that have previously funded organizations and are looking to fund ones that do what you're doing. If the organization has supported organizations that provide similar programs to yours, they're more than likely to be a potential funder to your organization.

Funders generally approve funding for organizations that have well-written proposals and/or organizations that:

- Share the same mission as the potential funder

- Programs help solve a problem the potential funder is passionate about

- Your organization's target population aligns with those the potential funder is passionate about

- Are in the same geographic area as the funder. Some funders, even though they may align with your mission, may only fund organizations in a particular city and/or state.

It's recommended that organizations start seeking small foundations at their state level to start with and then move onto searching grant directories. When accessing directories, you will realize most foundation directories house funding for all foundations that are grant-making entities. You may be able to find a few via a Google search. In the past, I've also been fortunate to find potential funders through other nonprofit servicing entities. I've signed up to receive the newsletters of these entities, which in turn would inform me when there's an open grant cycle sponsored by potential funders they're partnered with.

Aside from the few that I could access as a result of the aforementioned methods, that was not sufficient for long term sustainability. Therefore, we began to pay to access grant directories. In order to have access, you must sign up for membership (which has a fee attached to it). There are entities like Foundation Center, Grantwatch, and Candid.org, just to name a few. We use Grantwatch, which is $199.00 per year to utilize and very user friendly. Although it houses tons of foundation grants, you can narrow your search so that you're accessing potential funders that align with your mission and target population.

What does it mean to be grant ready?

No matter the flexibility or ease of foundation grants, an organization must still be grant ready in order to qualify or receive funding from a foundation. When I encounter founders and directors of nonprofit organizations, some are new to the space, and some are not. However, they are still not grant ready. I've found most founders to be extremely passionate about their mission and HELPING PEOPLE, but they have no idea how to structure their organization so that they can secure funding to do just that.

Although most of them want grants, their organizations are 1. Not positioned to receive granting, and 2. They don't have anyone on their team to assist in the grant writing space to secure ongoing funding for their organization. Grant readiness is an organization's ability to research, apply for, win, and manage grant applications successfully. Although most organizations think they're grant ready, the reality is that many don't have structured programs developed or other key essentials in place to assure they're ready and can handle grants. This is especially true of new organizations.

One of the first qualifying factors to receive grant funding is having a 501c3 Status.

In my business, we used to provide grant writing services. This meant we received tons of referrals for people that wanted a grant. One of the first questions I'd was, "do you have a nonprofit organization? Does it have a 501c3 status?" You wouldn't believe the number of people convinced they can qualify for a grant without even having a business.

I've had several individuals with for-profit businesses and had to inform them that the business has to be structured as a nonprofit and have a 501c3 status to qualify for grant funding.

The 501c3 application is rather straightforward. You have two choices: the 1023 EZ application (which is for organizations that will generate less than 50K in the first three years of existence) or the 1023 long form (for organizations that will exceed that amount).

Once you've completed your supporting documents for your organization, you complete the application that applies to you and wait to secure your status to apply for grant funding.

In the meantime, while waiting for your status to return, I encourage directors to implement their fund-raising plan to start generating funds from other sources, allowing the organization to get off to a wonderful start.

Clearly defined mission and purpose:

Before an organization applies for grant funding, it must have a clearly defined mission statement and vision. They must also be able to articulate the organization's purpose clearly.

Your mission should be unique to your organization, its work, and the target population your organization will be servicing. Your vision should be unique and specify what you plan to accomplish. Foundations will not fund organizations that duplicate or overlap similar services in their geographic area. Your mission must also be doable--saving the world won't work.

Company's history and description

Each nonprofit organization's Director should have a description of their organization that includes its history, the reason for existing, the mission and vision of the organization, the target population, and it's past and anticipated accomplishments.

You will also need to include some history of the organization, including how the organization was derived and the history of the founder. The history typically gives the backstory of how the organization originated.

Clearly defined programs and services

- Many founders will know the services they want to provide but won't have them compiled into a program. You must implement a measurable program (12-week program, 1-year program, etc.) that you can prove will make a difference to the individuals you are providing services to. Also, assure them that the program is one that will compel your target audience to attend and complete the program.

- Research-based data that demonstrates a need for their programs/services and how it will be beneficial to the target population in which they will be providing services to is also essential.

- Have a description of programs/services that includes goals and objectives, activities, key staff members, how the program/service will be evaluated, and any successes so far (if the program/service has already been implemented).

Adequate staff and involved Board of Directors

- Does your organization have capable leadership? You need qualified staff and an active board. An experienced CEO and a supportive board that's willing to assist with fundraising and sustain the nonprofit organization are essential.

- The organization will also need adequate staff to administer its programs and assure the success of them.

- You will need to have people (staff or consultants) and time to successfully manage the grant application process and write quality grant proposals. Although an organization that's just starting may not have a full-time grant writer on staff (due to the lack of funding), they should have one they at least contract with that can constantly compete for grant funding. Due to grant writing demands, it is best to have that as the focal point for an employee.

Financial Stability

- In regard to nonprofit organizations, many founders come into the nonprofit space, thinking grants are the end-all-be-all to funding their nonprofit organizations.

Nonprofits must have a fundraising plan that displays diverse revenue streams, and none should be heavily focused on grant funding.

Foundations want to be reassured that you don't have all of your eggs in one basket--especially theirs. They want to be sure you're not solely relying on grant funding.

- Have a financial sustainability plan that shows the financial stability of the organization. This plan should spell out: the organization's plan to financially sustain the organization with fundraisers, the strategy to secure sponsorships, partnerships for in-kind donations, earned income streams, etc. Potential funders know that you won't be able to sustain your work from grants alone. Therefore, you need to know this as well.

Strategic Planning-

- On an annual basis, corporations and businesses typically do what's called a SWOT Analysis. I recommend nonprofits to do the same. This will help the founder and Board to determine what's working and not working in the organization. They can utilize the survey to determine client satisfaction, as well as other measures to determine the effectiveness of the program being offered.

- Seek out other nonprofits to collaborate on the project you propose to a foundation. This is especially useful if you are a newer nonprofit. Collect letters of support from community leaders and organizations.

- Establish community partnerships with corporations and other businesses in the community to assist in strengthening the grant. Grantmakers know that one individual can't do everything. Partnerships will strengthen the grant writing process and increase the likelihood of the organization fulfilling its mission. This is because there are other entities involved to support the service provided to clients.

When an organization has implemented the aforementioned steps, it will help organizations be more competitive for grants. It's so much more than just helping people. Directors, you need money to do all that you want to do. Therefore, start positioning yourselves accordingly before seeking grants, and you will be able to use the same background information to assist with securing ongoing funding from other sources. Stay persistent nonprofits! What you're offering is needed!!!

SJ Stephens

FB: SJS. Business Building and More

Website: https://www.sjsbusinessbuilding.com

Instagram: sjs_businessbuilding

Email: Info@sjsbusinessbuilding.com

SJ Stephens is the Founder of SJS. Business Building & More; a Business Consulting Agency specializing in Grant Writing, business funding strategies, and business start-ups, amongst other things. She is the Lead Grant Writer for A.L.I.V.E. (Always Living in Victory Enterprises) and sits on the Grant Review Committee for FLOURISH/Generate Health.

Since founding SJS Business Building & More in June 2020, she has built a client base that expands over eight states and two foreign countries, with the furthest being in Haiti. SJ obtained her Bachelor of Science in Criminal Justice (2007) and her Master of Science in Criminal Justice Administration (2009). In 2010, she joined and graduated from the St. Louis Metropolitan Police Academy and served in the capacity of a St. Louis City, 7th District Officer. Over time, she discovered that her heart was in providing direct service to those in need and changed career paths.

Over the past four years, she has served in leadership positions with three major nonprofit organizations in the City of St. Louis while earning her Community Health Worker certification.

In November 2020, SJ launched her t-shirt line under the moniker "Big Jizzel" and her 1st self-published book, <u>Business Affirmations for Bosses</u>, which sold out (115 copies) in 31 hours. In 2021, she will open *R. Haley's Haven*, a Domestic Violence Safe Haven in remembrance of her bonus baby, Rashauwn Haley. Visit www.sjsbusinessbuilding.com to learn more.

When you are the Founder/CEO of a nonprofit organization, money is a thing...a HUGE thing. Everything from how to provide the services your community needs, to paying the light bill, all the way down to having the funds to buy office supplies are things that most startups do not have money for in the beginning. Of course, you can use your personal funds or take out small business loans. In reality, who wants to tie up their personal funds or credit?

As I transitioned from writing grants strictly for large, established nonprofit organizations to smaller, up and coming organizations, I have learned that many people start nonprofits and truly have no idea how to obtain the proper level of funding needed to start and sustain it. There is a horrible misconception that grants are easy to obtain, readily available, and all that one needs to do is apply (no matter the type of business they have). Then poof, they will be given money to run their business and pay themselves a salary right out of the gate. That is the furthest thing from reality.

Some of my initial clients had no idea what it took to run a nonprofit, let alone how to fund one. They struggled with the basic foundational questions such as do you have a DUNS number?

Do you have a business banking account? Do you have a budget? Do you have a mission statement? These are questions that they did not have answers for or were expecting me, the grant writer, to provide for them. The number of individuals who did not have a mission statement or even know what a mission statement was, was heartbreaking. People fail to realize that without having a direction for your organization, you are more than likely going nowhere.

Funding a nonprofit organization is not what I would describe as difficult, but there is a high level of advanced preparation that must be taken. I tell all of my clients that if you take the time to lay the proper foundation, everything else will ebb and flow the way it needs to; you must PREPARE. The average grant writer charges $25 per hour to prepare a grant application (this amount varies depending on the level of experience).

Imagine hiring a writer and having none of your documentation in order prior to the meeting. You are then being charged $25 an hour to do things that you could have done yourself. The entire grant readiness process can take anywhere from 15-25 hours (if you have not done your groundwork). That is not including the actual writing and submission of your grant application

The goal is to come to the table with your foundation and pay your writer to craft an amazing proposal--and nothing else. In this chapter, I will provide you with a basic grant readiness checklist to help guide you through the process. By no means is this list comprehensive; depending on your geographical location and even the type of grant funding you are seeking, there will always be additional steps required. This will cover all of the basics.

*At the end of the checklist, you will see a brief glossary of commonly used terms.

SJ Stephens Grant readiness checklist

Step one: The Foundation

1.   Is your organization a legally established entity? Do you have the following:

❏   A legally available name for your organization? You want to make sure that no other organization is using that name and that no entity holds the copyright to your name of preference. Simple, free name searches can be conducted on https://howtostartanllc.com/missouri-llc-name-search or https://www.uspto.gov.

2.   Have you applied for your domain name and business email? Nothing screams "startup" more than a Gmail, Hotmail, or Yahoo account attached to your business.

3.   Have you applied for and received the following:

- ❑ 501(c)3 tax-exempt status/IRS letter of determination

- ❑ IRS 990

- ❑ NAICS number (North American Industry Classification System)

- ❑ DUNs number

4.   Do you have a business banking account? This **HAS** to be separate from your personal account. For year-end tax transparency, your personal finances **MUST** be separate from your business finances.

5.   Do you have a business plan? What will your business look like in year one? How do you plan to expand in year two? What will your business look like in year five?

6.   What does your strategic timeline look like?

Step Two: Program Description

1.   Do you have a mission and vision statement?

2.   What is the motivation behind this organization?

3.   What are the core values of your organization?

4.   What is the community need/problem that your organization
seeks to address? Having actual statistics/data is very important. It is
one thing to state your opinion on why something is an issue and how
you feel it needs to be addressed; that is totally different than being
able to justify those statements. **DO YOUR RESEARCH!** You
absolutely **need the numbers!!**

5.   How will your organization address this need/problem?

6.   Who is your target population?

7.   What makes your organization different than others; what sets
you apart?

Step Three: Goals and Objectives

1.   What are your SMART goals and objectives? There is a
difference between goals and objectives; you need to be able to make
the distinction.

2.   What are your clear, desired, and realistic outcomes?

3. How will your objectives, goals, and outcomes be measured?

4. What program evaluation tools are you using? If they are not already in place, what do you intend to use? Have you done any research or trials on what works best for your program?

Step Four: Key Personnel

1. Who are you, and what makes you qualified to do this work? Be prepared to provide your resume and a summary of your professional background and experience.

2. Do you have a proven track record of doing this type of work?

3. Who sits on your Board of Directors, and how are they affiliated within the community?

4. Who are the key players in your organization, what are their titles, what is their job description, and how are they qualified? Be prepared to submit updated resumes for everyone with a title in your organization.

5. Is your organizational hierarchy in place?

6. Who are your community collaborators and/or partnerships? If you do not have any, why not? Is there no one in your community addressing this need, or have you simply chosen not to work with them?

Step Five: Knowing your needs

1.   Do you have a financial statement? This will only apply if you have been in business for longer than twelve months.

2.   Do you have an itemized, board-approved annual operating budget?

3.   What funding streams are you prepared to explore? Do you want only grants? Are you willing to fundraise? Do you have personal funds? Are you interested in crowd funding? Sponsorships? Private donors?

3.   What is your sustainability plan?

***This is the single most important question throughout this document. In addition to being a Grant Writer, I sit on a grant approval committee as well.

One of the first questions that come up anytime we have a funding request from a start-up organization is how will they be able to keep the doors open next year if we are not able to fund them again? We turn down a significant number of otherwise qualified applicants simply because they could not articulate a long-term financial plan. Not too many funders are willing to pour money into a project that won't last past the fiscal year.* * *

4.   Will you require your Board of Directors to make annual financial contributions?

5.   Have you already applied for grants and been awarded? If so, from who, how much, and when? Always, always, always keep track of who you receive money from. This should be a running spreadsheet.

Step Six: Marketing and Promotion

1.   Does your organization currently have a social media presence? What will your funders think if they go and take a look? Is it professional? Does it provide accurate information about your organization? Is it visually appealing?

2.   What marketing tools will you use to attract and engage with your clients?

Step Seven: Miscellaneous items

1.   Do you have a solicitation proposal?

2.   Do you have recent letters of support?

3.   If you cannot afford a staff, have you looked into utilizing volunteers? Practicum students? AmeriCorp VISTAS?

I hope you find this list beneficial. Please understand, I am not saying that you cannot apply for grants without all of the information listed above or that it is not okay to seek professional help putting this list together. This list is simply to be used as a guide to streamline your process and save you money in the end. The overall goal is to GET money, not spend it unnecessarily.

Commonly used terms:

- 501c3 organization- A corporation, trust, unincorporated association, or another type of organization that is fully exempt from paying federal taxes.

- Board of Directors-The governing body of the organization.

- Business plan- A detailed outline of your organization's objectives and strategies for achieving them.

- **Crowdfunding**-Funding conducted via the internet that raises small amounts of money from a large number of people.

- **DUNS number**-A unique nine-character number used to identify an organization. This number is used to track funds received from federal funding streams, contracts, and private foundations. This number is used to access your business credit information, including (but not limited to) your business credit rating, legal judgments, and payment history.

- **IRS 990**-The annual form that tax-exempt organizations must file that provides the IRS with an overview of the organization and its detailed financial information.

- **Mission statement**- Describes the purpose of an organization.

- **NAICS code**- A self-assigned code selected by your organization that describes the primary business activity being conducted.

- **SMART goals**- SMART is an acronym for Specific, Measurable, Achievable, Relevant, and Time-based. These five elements help create your organization's goals in a thoughtfully planned out manner that is easy to track.

- **Solicitation letter**-A letter written to potential donors/sponsors/funders that explains briefly what your organization needs and why. These letters usually have an emotional pull, but at the same time are very direct and genuine in their asking.

- **Strategic plan**- A statement that helps pair your organizational objectives with the needs of the community. Your strategic plan should include processes, inputs, outputs, and desired outcomes.

- **Sustainability**-The ability to maintain a certain rate or level over a certain amount of time.

- **Vision statement**- Describes the goals of an organization.

- **Operating budget**- An estimate of all annual income and expenses your organization will have over a set amount of time. Usually, most funders want to see an annual budget (12 months).

Michael and Faith Thomas

Facebook: m.facebook.com/masaourathomas

Profiles: profile.blue/michael-m-thomas

Website: www.michaelandfaith.com

Email: info@michaelandfaith.com

Michael and Faith Thomas are independent nonprofit development and grant writing consultants dedicated to assisting organizations and individuals with achieving exponential growth. This duo (and their team) provide the answers people need to develop programming and projects that are qualified for grant funding.

Michael Thomas, a native of Danville, Virginia, has been active in providing services for groups and philanthropic leaders for over twenty years. He inspires and energizes diverse audiences and provides training for novice and experienced organizations to grow and excel. As a former Real Estate Broker that has worked extensively with statistics and demographics, Mr. Thomas masterfully relates personal instinct and strategic planning to address marketplace needs with timely solutions. After receiving a bachelor's degree from the Jacksonville Theological Bible College, Mr. Thomas dedicated his life to helping others achieve their highest potential, which quickly grew into assisting leaders in developing themselves and their teams to maximize their capacity.

Faith Thomas, a native of Hertford, NC, is a corporate veteran with over two decades of experience in financial services, business analytics, training facilitation, process development, and business consultation. As a graduate of North Carolina Agricultural and Technical State University, Mrs. Thomas harnessed the skills of research and intellectual presentation, which provided a platform to matriculate to Assistant Vice President of a Fortune 500 company. While there, she gained experience in leading teams, developing processes, and facilitated risk-based training, including executive-level employees in North Carolina, Delaware, New York, Arizona, and California.

As a married couple of nearly 20 years, Michael and Faith share a passion for philanthropic work. From the start of their marriage, the duo became involved in community outreach. They lead diverse teams to serve thousands of people with food, clothing, toiletries, resource connections, workshops, acts of kindness events, and messages of hope.

Their desire to expand their work led to the founding of Propel Forward, Inc., a 501 (c) (3) tax-exempt nonprofit organization aimed at assisting individuals who face challenges due to poverty, displacement, and lack of resources.

The organization's foundation includes the connection of local resources, which led the team into nonprofit consulting. To expand their hands-on knowledge of program development and grant writing, the team joined a group of consultants that helped local organizations, community colleges, universities, and churches to gain over three hundred million dollars in cash grant awards.

Based in Winston-Salem, NC, Michael and Faith Thomas provide nonprofit consulting, grant writing training, administrative training, and grant writing services for nonprofit organizations and churches. Through the power of communication and information, this duo is dedicated to impacting the world, one strategy and one awarded grant at a time.

For more information or to receive consulting services, visit www.michaelandfaith.com.

TEAM POWER

One of the most impressive events in sports history is the 2016 Olympic-Women's four by one hundred meters relay. With precision and speed, Allyson Felix, English Gardner, Tianna Bartoletta, and Tori Bowie performed as an unmatched team and defeated the best in the world by bringing home the coveted gold medal. Their historic win as a team was quite spectacular for millions of fans, especially when victory seemed impossible after the heart-breaking qualifying round.

During the qualifier, a Brazilian runner encumbered the second exchange baton pass between Felix and Gardner and caused Team USA to finish last in their heat. The race was protested and resulted in the relay-team being allowed to complete a special run. Alone on the track without the adrenaline of an opponent, the team astounded the world by not only unseating China but obtained the number one qualifying time of 41.77 seconds. With palpable focus and determination, the four Olympians advanced to the final race and achieved the prize they were unmistakably prepared to win.

As in the sport of Track and Field, there is fierce competition amongst charitable organizations for grant funding. However, rather than having the benefit of a group's effort, like a track team, many nonprofit organizations and churches operate with a solo person when seeking grant funding. This singular approach can become quite expensive when paying someone to apply for funding year after year. It can become overwhelming and cause burn out when only one or two people shoulder the tasks of continually writing grant proposals to support an organization's efforts.

As grant service professionals, it is Michael and Faith Thomas's goal to see charitable entities save money, reduce stress, and sustain a financially healthy organization through the process of establishing a grant team. A grant team is comprised of a group of individuals who have an interest in creating competitive grant applications to ensure the successful implementation of an organization's program. The composition of a grant team can vary; however, there are five key roles Michael and Faith recommend for the creation of credible, attractive, and compelling grant proposals.

These roles are identified as the Grant Team Leader, Data Collector, Budget Developer, Community Liaison, and the Writer-Editor. Each role plays an integral part in submitting great grant proposals. The process of getting to know the grant funder, adhering to the grant guidelines, and highlighting the organization's mutual interest requires extreme focus and determination. It is best executed by a dedicated team that is trained, prepared, and ready to win.

THE TEAM LEAD

The team leader's role within a grant team is comparative to a project manager. It requires the skill sets seen in strong administrators, great motivators, and leaders who are resourceful and relentless in making sure the organization's funding goals are reached. Much like a track coach, the Team Leader has the foresight needed to accomplish the goal. This type of coach is vested in making sure the group works as one well-oiled machine while also motivating each person to perform at their highest potential.

Throughout this chapter, you will understand that as each grant team member completes the assigned tasks, the completed work is passed on to the next person.

This passing of the baton to the next team member requires smooth transitions.

The grant team leader must plan for the success of each person's role and ensure all tasks are handed off smoothly. The team leader may also be responsible for identifying grant opportunities, facilitating team meetings, assigning tasks, monitoring progress, and submitting the final draft of a grant proposal. Because there are multiple hats that a grant lead wears, it is recommended that nonprofits and churches select a lead with close ties to the organization. Typically, for small nonprofit organizations, the executive director serves as the grant team lead.

The executive director carries the vision of the organization and has the ear of the governing board. He or she will also be responsible for significant components of the grant, such as obtaining community support letters and signing the necessary documents associated with the grant proposal. The lead's dedication and passion for seeing the organization's programs funded should be apparent and evident. The success of the nonprofit and its ability to be financially solvent must be paramount.

Consequently, the executive director is the most probable and suitable match for handling the role of leading the grant team, particularly for organizations whose annual operating budget is less than two hundred and fifty thousand dollars. Keeping a grant team energized and motivated can become difficult if the lead does not have a strong desire to see the program funded. Luke-warm affinities for the work and services of the organization can be the missing link in crafting winning grant proposals.

Since the team leader is responsible for supporting the team to achieve positive results, the lead should also receive support for their efforts. As organizations become financially solvent, the administrative budget should include a line item to pay for a grant leader's service. By placing value and investing in the team leader, charitable groups will equip their grant writing team with the tenacity needed to achieve success.

Grant Prospecting is another responsibility that can be assigned to the grant writing team lead. Grant Prospecting includes researching various foundations, corporations, and governmental groups' giving cycles and histories.

Depending on the scope and uniqueness of the project or program, the team leader can spend hours upon hours utilizing search engines such as the Foundation Directory Online, Philanthropy News Digest, and Fluxx Grantseeker. There are thousands of organizations dedicated to funding efforts that match its mission. Because of the seemingly overwhelming options and deadlines to request financial support, it is highly recommended that a grant lead create a calendar to properly strategize the best use of the team's time and resources. In addition to the team leader's ability to identify funding opportunities, the lead should also devise a plan to mobilize the team to present outstanding and attractive proposals on a continual basis.

The mobilization of the team includes facilitating consistent grant writing meetings, where the team leader will brief the group about the financial goals of each program and the strategy to reach each funding goal. Having reviewed the Program Logic Model, the leader will assign the team members the tasks that are deemed necessary to communicate a compelling grant proposal.

The team leader will serve as a project manager and clearly communicate the details of the timeline and schedule checkpoints for each team member. The purpose of the checkpoints is to monitor and track the progress of the assigned tasks while also providing motivational support, tools, and resources that each grant writing team member may need. This individual attention must be balanced with promoting a team atmosphere, where the group understands the importance of the role they serve yet consistently receive a reminder that reaching the goal must be a collective effort. The common phrase that a chain is only as strong as its weakest link should become an ideology of the grant writing team leader. The leader should be dedicated to making sure this pattern of thought is communicated and reinforced as the team collaborates together.

THE DATA COLLECTOR

The Data Collector is the first to hold the baton in the race to win a grant award. Commonly known as the "Researcher," the data collector is responsible for ensuring the program's need has been established through empirical evidence and statistical data.

Every charitable organization should be able to communicate clearly and succinctly the problem that is being solved through its programs and services. This ability to effectively communicate how the problem is being addressed establishes Social Return on Investment (SROI). SROI is a principled method of measuring the impact that typically does not include value creation in a commercial market. For benevolent organizations, the non-financial value should be outlined in its objectives and convey how the goal of societal progress will be implemented through its programming.

Foundations, Corporations, and Government entities that offer grant awards would like to be convinced of how their monetary support will assist the program's impact on specific social ills or the opportunities for advancement and progress. These grant funders want to confirm who they are helping, why they need help, and what the results are when help is given. Moreover, many funders look for concrete evidence of the community's actual desire to receive, or willingness to participate in, the services being offered by the organization requesting monetary support.

The data collector is a key team member whose role is to connect the need to the solution, provide assurance of a positive social return, and verify the program is wanted and will be utilized by the community it serves. Consequently, the skills required for this role include critical analysis (with the ability to understand social and cultural contexts through data), an attentiveness for details, recognition of credible sources, and patience for tedious tasks.

To identify a need, the data collector should conduct research that clearly outlines the *problem* and the *need*. When possible, the information gathered to highlight the *problem* should relate to national, state, and local statistics to emphasize why the program benefits the community it serves. For example, if the nonprofit or faith-based organization has a community garden program to address reducing obesity, the Data Collector would look for data that verifies obesity is a problem for the population of people the community garden is designed to help.

After the problem is authenticated, the data collector would then research supporting information on why the community garden is expected to reduce the problem.

A credible source such as the National Institute of Health (NIH) could provide the information a researcher would need for this topic. In 2015, the NIH published an article outlining how the lack of access to healthy foods (food deserts) explains why residents of low-income neighborhoods in the U.S have high rates of obesity. Using local data, the data collector would then quantify how its target demographic qualifies as a food desert and the number of people who suffer from obesity; therefore, making the connection between the *need* for a community garden that will provide healthy food and consequently help reduce the *problem* of obesity.

In addition to ascertaining the existence of a problem, the Data Collector can strengthen a grant proposal by locating the information that supports how the program will have other residual benefits. In the community garden example, additional findings such as the increase in personal savings can connect the dots between the need and a broader social benefit. The following paragraphs are an example of how to develop a broader benefit of a community garden project.

According to the 2017 "Losing Weight Can Save You a Lot of Money" Esquire article, a Johns Hopkins Bloomberg School of Public Health study noted the amount of money saved when adults move from being obese to a healthier weight. The article stated that a twenty-year-old adult could save $28,020, a thirty-year-old saves $27,331, a forty-year-old saves $31,447, and at age fifty, the savings peak at $36,278. Forbes 2017 September publication also noted these findings and related how taxes, insurance premiums, and the economy connects everyone.

To make a distinct point, Forbes noted that extra weight eventually costs everyone. Using credible sources to paint a broader picture, the data collector can gather the information that will show the parallels between an individual being helped to the whole of society being helped. These types of connections create a strong and compelling pitch for grant funding. The data collector should work very closely with the team leader to ensure they do not become overwhelmed with the seemingly unending realms of information that is available when researching an issue or potential opportunity.

This first leg of the race must rely on the coach to have clear instructions concerning the purpose of the program. Although additional benefits may be discovered during the research phase, the Data Collector must apply discipline and create a trail that leads from the *problem* to the solution.

Along with proving the need from credible research sources, the Data Collector may also receive the task of verifying the community's willingness to partake in the services being offered. This task can be accomplished through surveys and forums. Canvasing the community in person or utilizing an online survey are two ways to prove need and commitment. Would you like to participate in this program? Are you willing to pay a five-dollar registration fee? Would you volunteer two hours a week, are all examples of appropriate survey questions. From the responses, the Data Collector can provide the information needed to assure the grant funder the cash awarded for the program is a wise investment. Such data conveys the number of people the organization has planned to service and the number of volunteers who will provide the service.

Additionally, the data collector may be assigned to track the performance of a program that has been in operation for at least two to three months. Metrics that were established in the Program Logic Model can be used as the standard to determine if the program's activities are having a positive impact. This information will be vital in conveying the value of continuing the service. Retrieving quarterly results is an excellent routine the collector can incorporate to build reports and graphs that could show results and impact within a proposal.

Once the data collector has strategically connected the need to the solution, highlighted the SROI, verified the program would be utilized, and noted the current impact, the baton can be passed to the next member of the grant team, the budget administrator.

THE BUDGET ADMINISTRATOR

Unlike the second leg of a relay race, which is typically not viewed as the most crucial position on the team, the budget administrator is paramount to making a clear case for why the grant proposal is being submitted. The skill sets associated with this role include thinking critically, meeting deadlines, and exercising a proficient use concerning the creation and maintenance of data spreadsheets. Accountants, business analysts, and other financial services professionals are great candidates to complete the tasks of the budget administrator's role. However, anyone willing to serve in this position can be trained in a relatively short amount of time to fill this important responsibility on the team.

Knowing the exact amount needed to operate and manage a project, along with outlining the specific amount of money and resources required to execute services, is crucial to presenting a sound grant proposal. Therefore, the budget administrator should be extremely comfortable forecasting revenue and expenditures for a set period of time.

They should work closely with the organization's treasurer to verify the amount of money being allotted for a program, and verifying all known expenses related to operations is an expectation of this role. Like all other team members, the budget administrator must be clear about the organization's purpose and the details of the program's activities. A pitfall for many grant writing teams occurs when the budget does not accurately reflect the financial needs associated with providing services to the community. Without the ability to compare current revenue with forecasted expenses, the grant proposal will be ineffective in proving its need for additional funding support.

For example, if the nonprofit or faith-based organization receives $50,000.00 annually, and its program's budget has expenses of only $35,000.00, then a grant review board will be unclear about why a grant application is being submitted. The organization appears to have a surplus of $15,000.00. This type of discrepancy lends to the opinion that the organization is fiscally irresponsible. It also casts doubt that grant funding is truly needed.

It is up to the budget administrator to outline (with extreme detail) all program expenses, administrative costs, and other operating commitments. For accuracy, the budget administrator will need to price the goods and services required to implement or manage the program. In conjunction with pricing, the administrator should forecast inflation costs. From office supplies to a general contractor's fee, the budget administrator should account for every range of expenses, big or small. Such details should be used to create and maintain a statement of activities, which will allow the grant team to showcase the financial status and identify the charitable organization's needs.

Additionally, the budget administrator should prepare a future sustainability plan. A sustainability plan allows the grant funder to understand the path the organization is taking to become financially solvent with minimum grant support needed in the future. This plan's development will require the administrator to work closely with the executive director to reflect on how future efforts will convert into dollars and in-kind contributions, which will fund the charitable services.

The financial health of an organization may rise or fall based on the ability of the entity to communicate sources of revenue and details of expenses effectively. The budget administrator holds one of the major keys to providing credibility concerning the ask for funding. With a job well done by the budget administrator, the next team member can grab the baton to do their part to help prepare a stellar grant proposal.

THE COMMUNITY LIAISON

Much like the third leg of a relay race, the community liaison is the grant team's slowest member. The speed at which this person operates does not diminish the value of this role. The sheer nature and function of this position require a slow approach because it entails discovering information and forging essential partnerships; these tasks should not be rushed.

Using the data provided by the data collector and the budget administrator, the community liaison scouts for local opportunities and initiatives that will enhance the soundness and quality of the grant proposal.

The grant team's liaison should be a friendly person who is not intimidated by the responsibility of introducing themselves to strangers or shining a positive spotlight on the organization at local events and municipal meetings on a consistent basis. Central places such as the City Council, Chamber of Commerce, and Board of Education meetings are frequently scheduled gatherings that discuss local, state, and federal funding available to community-focused organizations.

Many people who lead or attend these types of meetings also serve on grant review boards and have information concerning how a charitable program can best position itself to request funding. A nonprofit or faith-based organization can discover valuable information that may not be widely known or advertised by having a presence within the community. For example, city councils often decide to provide workshops to properly complete grant applications for upcoming funding that is being offered by the city. This type of early knowledge affords an extra advantage in the grant writing process, and the Community Liaison can help achieve this benefit.

Another benefit of being an integral voice in the community is forming partnerships with other civic, educational, or business groups that can enhance a program or service. Community Liaisons can be the loudest cheerleaders for nonprofits or faith-based groups. They possess the savvy to bring public awareness to the organization's work, solidifying partnerships. Collaboration is a buzz word in the grant world. When charitable groups show strong collaborations, the program is more compelling as a grant worthy investment.

For example, a nonprofit in Winston-Salem, North Carolina, was challenged with retaining volunteers. While attending a local event hosted by the Urban League, the Community Liaison met one of the event planners and discovered another organization whose purpose was to funnel paid personnel to nonprofits who cannot afford to pay salaries for people to work with its community-based program. This type of partnership is a win-win for both organizations and exhibits the stability of the program. Such collaborations help to enhance nonprofits and elevate the potential to compete with complementary programs for the same grants.

In preparing a grant proposal, quality information and collaborations are significant in the organization to showcase its attractive and compelling programming. Forging relationships and building partnerships take time and consistency. Even when a grant is not in the process of being written, the community liaison is at work to steadily build the organization's reputation and credibility. This groundwork is astoundingly beneficial and positions the next team member to take the baton to produce a winning grant proposal.

THE WRITER & EDITOR

The final position in a relay race is called the anchor leg. This team member is typically the fastest and has the most experience. This person is responsible for making up ground or preserving the lead handed to them by their teammates. In either circumstance, the anchor is expected to secure the win. The writers and editors are the MVPs of the grant writing team. Because the writer and editor skill sets are almost identical, they operate as one unit on the team.

As the anchor of a relay team, they too are expected to recoup lost ground or capitalize from any given lead to obtain grant awards.

Consequently, the writer-editor should be well versed in how the information provided by the data collector, budget administrator, and community liaison should be used to prepare a proposal with the purpose of persuading grant review boards to provide financial support. The end-product must reflect the plan to advance a worthwhile cause and prove that the nonprofit or faith-based organization is responsible and capable of executing the plan.

The writer-editor should have proficient writing skills with a strong competency in sentence structure and grammar usage. They should be detail-oriented and able to communicate well with teammates. Reading comprehension is paramount, following directions is key, and the ability to connect the dots between the data, the execution plan, and the expected results are necessary skills. It starts with the Writer reviewing the Request for Proposal (RFP) or Request for Application (RFA) to identify what information the grantor is asking for.

The writer will pay strict attention to precisely follow the funder's directions to ensure they do not provide less than what was requested. Likewise, they will reframe from providing additional information to violate any parameters or restrictions the grantor put in place. For example, suppose the funder asks that proposals are limited to 5 pages. In that case, even if the writer has 12 pages of information, the priority must be to follow the guidelines and honor the funder's request.

After verifying the specifics within the RFP or RFA, the writer will diligently outline the proposal's layout and then begin applying the best practices of preparing a winning grant proposal. The writer will decide how to strategically convey the purpose, activities, and results of the program and skillfully place charts, graphs, maps, and other appropriate visuals previously provided by teammates to craft a compelling narrative.

The editor works in conjunction with the writer as a second eye to ensure the content of the proposal is logical. The editor will also check for grammatical errors, such as the use of an inappropriate verb tense or a misplaced modifier.

Additionally, this team member can offer suggestions to rephrase the content to ensure the information's placement and flow is clear, concise, and meets the requirements of the grantor's request. Together, the writer and editor will work hand in hand to produce a grant proposal that meets and hopefully exceeds the grant funder's expectations. Because of the meticulous considerations these roles take in submitting a grant application, the entire team is positioned to cross the finish line and achieve a well-deserved win.

TEAM POWER MULTIPLIED

Henry Ford once said, "Coming together is the beginning. Staying together is progress and working together is success." These words ring true when attempting to build a coalition of like-minded individuals who offer their time, resources, and talents to serve others. By creating a grant writing team, nonprofit and faith-based organizations will not only benefit financially, but they also provide an avenue for many others to serve their community in a specific capacity.

Like any great team, duplicating the role of the data collector, budget administrator, community liaison, writer, and editor is a recipe for success and is a recommended goal for charitable organizations. Sharing the load in preparing grant proposals gives team members the flexibility to rotate responsibilities and avoid burnout.

Organizations want to avoid the pitfall of team members dropping the proverbial baton, which can be avoided by duplicating as many grant team roles as possible. Recruiting understudies, substitutes, and back-up team members as a shared ideology can offer opportunities to involve more people in the work of providing valuable programs and services to various communities throughout the nation. This multiplying power is a magnificent key that can be used to unlock grant funding doors.

TEAM THOMAS

Michael and Faith Thomas are dedicated to empowering organizations throughout the nation in becoming financially solvent entities. This duo can help your organization or church develop grant worthy programs and build grant writing teams to achieve sustainable growth through consultation and several training mechanisms. If you would like to know more about Michael and Faith Thomas and the services they provide, please visit www.michaelandfaith.com.

Jose Villa

Email: jose@villa-bc.com

Instagram: Villa_bc

Website: www.villa-bc.com

Mr. Villa was born and raised in New York City's Spanish Harlem. He enlisted in the Air Force at 17 and completed his 23-year Air Force Information Technology Officer career as a Major. He served seven years as an enlisted man, went to Officer Training School, and served 16 years as an officer. Having lived and worked in multi-ethnic, multicultural situations around the globe -- 7 years in Tokyo, two years in Taiwan, 18 months in Pakistan, and lived or worked in 27 states --he is comfortable in Hawaii's international business melting pot. He has lived there for 34 years. He also speaks Spanish (native speaker) and Mandarin Chinese (fairly fluently).

Mr. Villa has 25 years' experience as a nonprofit organization (NPO) and commercial business consultant. NPOs and businesses hire his company - *Villa Business Consulting* - for their writing projects. These include NPO grant proposals; business plans; 8(a) federal contractor certification applications; minority-owned, women-owned, and veteran-owned business national and federal certifications. The latter enables businesses to bid on government and corporate set-aside contracts.

He has a BSC in Marketing from Rider University (Lawrenceville, New Jersey), an M.A. in Government and Human Relations from Webster University (Webster Groves, Missouri), and a graduate certificate from the Air Command & Staff College (Montgomery, Alabama). Mr. Villa has served in various NPO capacities, including Executive Director (E.D.), Director of Marketing, Communications Director, and Senior Grant Writer. These positions included the role of E.D. of Honolulu Habitat for Humanity, deputy director of a 450-member NPO staff that managed 40 programs (spanning from 1,650 preschoolers (federal Head Start program) to an alternative GED for homeless and formerly incarcerated individuals), Pearl Harbor Aviation Museum grant writer, and Domestic Violence Action Center (Honolulu) grants' manager. These combined experiences have given him comprehensive respect for the inner workings of nonprofit organizations.

For nine years, Mr. Villa published the *Hawaii Hispanic News* – a 28-page, full-color, bilingual (English/Spanish) newspaper (1994-1999 and 2008-2012). From May 2006 to June 2012, he did weekly *"This Week in the Hispanic Nation"* news broadcasts on Hawaii Public Radio (HPR).

He also served as a guest commentator on HPR, and he was considered the "go-to guy" on issues involving Hawaii's diverse Hispanic communities. Mr. Villa was president of the Hawaii Hispanic Chamber of Commerce. He led the first one to the 1994 "Small Hispanic Chamber of the Year for the Western United States" award. In July 2007, he --and three other Hispanic business people -- co-founded Latin Business Hawaii, a Hispanic chamber. He also served on the Small Business Administration-Hawaii Advisory Board (14 years), the State Drug Abuse Commission (2 years), and Honolulu Federal Detention Center's Advisory Board (I year).

His awards include:

1)   1987: District 49 (State of Hawaii) International Speech Competition winner.

2)   1989: Served on the commission that established Dr. Martin Luther King, Jr. state holiday in Hawaii.

3)   1995: Hawaii Small Business Administration (SBA)'s "Small Business Advocate of the Year."

4)   2013: SBA State of Hawaii "Minority Small Business Champion of the Year."

5)   2013: SBA Region IX's (Arizona, California, Guam, Hawaii, and Nevada) "Minority Small Business Champion of the Year."

6)   2013: State of Hawaii Toastmasters' "Communication & Leadership Award."

Mr. Villa was a Toastmaster for ten years and keynote speaker at the 1998 Toastmasters International Western Regional Speech Competition. He has also been a guest presenter at Massachusetts Institute of Technology (MIT), Spark Matsunaga Institute for Peace, University of Hawaii Law School, University of Hawaii School of Journalism, Honolulu Media Council, Hawaii Pacific University, Pearl Harbor Naval Station, Hickam Air Force Base, Schofield Barracks, Wheeler Army Airfield, Tripler Army Medical Center, and SBA offices (Rochester, NY; Buffalo, NY; and Honolulu, HI).

His non-profit writing specialties include:

501(c) (3) applications; nonprofit grant proposals; and commercial or nonprofit business plans.

His for-profit writing specialties include these corporate and government certifications:

–   MBE (Minority Business Enterprise)

–   WBE (Woman Business Enterprise)

- VBE (Veteran Business Enterprise)

- SBA 8(a) Business Development Program

- VOSB (Veteran-Owned Small Business)

- WOSB (Woman-Owned Small Business)

- DBE (Disadvantaged Business Enterprise)

Background

I am a descendent of African slaves the Spaniards brought to Puerto Rico in the 1800s. My great-grandparents were undoubtedly slaves. My mother was part of the "Great Migration" of Puerto Ricans that fled the impoverished island after World War II. She settled in New York City's "Spanish Harlem," a mushrooming Puerto Rican neighborhood. I was born and raised there, so Spanish was my first language.

Back then, fat kids were considered healthy kids. I was so "healthy" I could not play sports. Nobody wanted a fat, unathletic kid on their team. So, I spent a lot of time in my room reading. I was fascinated by the English language. If I ran across a word I did not know, I would look it up in a dictionary. The thesaurus became a best friend.

During my teen years, we lived in the South Bronx, and I commuted to high school on 65th and Broadway (present site of Julliard School of Music). I always wanted to be a Marine. When I finally turned 17, I applied, but due to a slipped disk, I failed the Marine Corps' physical.

However, I scored high on the written exam and--to help mitigate my inconsolable disappointment--the Marine recruiter recommended I speak with the Air Force team. Their recruiter saw my scores and essentially said, "welcome to the Air Force, young man."

Of the 20 guys I grew up with, my homies, I was the only one that got out of Spanish Harlem on good terms. The rest were killed, got strung out on drugs, or went to prison. Conversely, I served 23 years in the Air Force and earned a bachelor's and master's degree while on active duty. I completed my service as a Major. Along the way, I lived seven years in Tokyo, two years in Taiwan, and 18 months in Pakistan; I lived or worked in 27 states, including Hawaii, my home for 34 years. I also became fairly fluent in a third language – Mandarin Chinese.

To this day, I credit reading and the Air Force with saving my life. Reflecting on where I came from, I walked some of the same paths as my homies. So, I could have been strung out on drugs or in prison today, or I might not have even had today. Instead, I have been blessed to be married to my beautiful wife, Mari, for 21 years. We have five kids, 14 grandchildren, and three great-grandchildren between us. So, I live a life of appreciation.

Grant Writing Genesis

I started writing grants in 1994 as a Hawaii Hispanic Chamber of Commerce board member. Those $1,000-$5,000 grants helped subsidize the executive team's attendance at annual Hispanic chamber conventions in various cities around the nation. That allowed our small chamber to connect with–and learn from–larger chambers.

I also started a one-page newsletter in 1994 that, over time, morphed into a 28-page, full-color newspaper called the *Hawaii Hispanic News*. My wife Mari and I published the newspaper for nine years. That gave us a journalism background, and Mari went on to be a college journalism instructor in upstate New York for four years.

In 1999, Honolulu Habitat for Humanity hired me as its Executive Director because I had grant writing experience. It was my first paid nonprofit organization (NPO) position, and I was thrilled at the opportunity. We had a two-person office. Two days after I started, my executive assistant went on 90-day maternity leave. At that point, I started reading every file in the jam-packed five-drawer file cabinet until I knew the NPO's 11-year history inside-out.

Since then, I have held several NPO positions, including Deputy Director (of a 450-staff member NPO with a $21M budget, 40 different programs, and 1,650 preschoolers in our federal Head Start Program); Director, Marketing & Communications; and Senior Grant Writer, but grant writing continued to be my favorite NPO passion.

Experience Portfolio Evolution

Over the years, Mari and I did freelance writing projects for clients across the nation in places like Rochester, NY; Buffalo, NY; Orlando, FL; Atlanta, GA; Montgomery, AL; Washington, D.C.; San Jose, CA; Philadelphia, PA; and Oahu, Maui, and Hawaii Islands, etc.

In 2007, Disney planned to build a resort in a Honolulu suburb and was looking for a local partner to co-sponsor M/WBE (Minority Business Enterprise and Woman Business Enterprise) certification workshops. Since Mari was president of our highly active Latin Business Hawaii (Hispanic chamber), the Chamber of Commerce of Hawaii recommended the Disney folks contact her.

We were both shocked and pleased when she got the call from Disney. We explained we had no experience with these certification programs but were willing to learn. They said their team would help guide us. We were impressed by the opportunity the programs provided entrepreneurs to grow their businesses by applying for corporate set-aside contracts. Besides, we were not about to pass up an opportunity to partner with Disney.

Our other workshop partners were the National Minority Supplier Diversity Council, Johnson Controls, and Wyndham Hotels. Workshop attendees were welcomed by our lieutenant governor. We have been doing small business certifications ever since.

In addition, we also learned the SBA 8(a) Business Development Program certification process; became proficient in the IRS 501(c)(3) application packages; and completed 140 business plans for a wide range of commercial enterprises. In 2016, after accompanying Mari during her professorship in Rochester for three years, we decided to move back home to Hawaii. I got a grant-writing position at a domestic violence NPO in Honolulu.

It was one of the most difficult jobs I ever had. Every day I saw victims in our reception area, and their pain was palpable. While I did not directly deal with them, I wrote some of their stories in grant applications; even that peripheral contact was painful. I experienced something called "vicarious trauma."

At my four-month point, the Pearl Harbor Aviation Museum advertised a grant writer position. The museum's primary missions are two-fold. They focus on commemorating the bombing of Pearl Harbor on December 7th, 1941, and acknowledging America's incredible resilience in coming together as a nation (eventually, defeating the attacker).

Based on my background in the Air Force and grant writing, I was thrilled to be offered the position. I was their in-house grant writer from October 2016 to February 2019. That position greatly improved my grant writing portfolio by exposing me to many "mainstream" grant writing opportunities, experiences, and practices.

Home-Based Business Launch

In the last few years, Mari and I had noticed, and advocated for, a paradigm shift in the NPO world from in-house grant writers to remote freelance contract grant writers. We felt NPOs benefitted from this in several ways, including higher productivity and fewer expenses (no need to pay benefits or provide in-house space, computer, desk, resources, etc.). However, most NPOs were stuck in the "old school" model and reluctant to trust "outsiders," but we saw occasional signs that this was changing.

In February 2019, Mari and I were in-house grant writers--she at the Honolulu YWCA and me at the aviation museum. We were so convinced remote grant writing was a viable full-time employment option that we decided to quit our jobs. We converted two bedrooms into our offices and started our own company working from home. Rather than just focus on nonprofits, we offered a diversified portfolio of services for small businesses as well.

We offered NPOs business plans, grant readiness assessments, 501c3 nonprofit applications, grant research, and grant writing. Our initial for-profit services included business plans, RFPs (Requests for Proposals), and national and government minority, women, and veteran-owned business certifications (including the preeminent Small Business Administration's 8(a) Business Development Program).

After about a week, the initial euphoria of having quit our jobs and launching our consultancy wore off and economic realities set in. We then had a horrible week of sleepless nights, focusing on the idiocy of both of us having simultaneously quit our jobs. How were we going to make it? What should we have done instead? Why hadn't we made a more strategic–and well-thought-out–transition? How could we be so dumb?

Then, on March 1, 2020, our first full-time day in business, Mari got a call from a long-time friend who owns one of Hawaii's largest public relations/marketing firms. She told Mari, "I have lost large contracts because my business is not certified. I do not understand what that means or how it is done. Is that what you guys do now?" Mari responded, "that is exactly what we do." Our friend replied, "then sign me up.

I want you to get my company certified." Ironically, she believed in us before we believed in ourselves. Knowing that someone of her caliber and stature had faith in us made a powerful difference; our business took off from there.

By the end of 2019, we had matched both our previous salaries working in t-shirts and shorts. When COVID-19 struck in March 2020, we were already adept at working remotely. And–ironically--our revenue stream has increased substantially since the pandemic began. Thanks to our having lived and worked in Hawaii for over 30 years, 90% of our new business is referred by existing or former clients. That has been a tremendous revelation, and we feel thankful/blessed every day.

The overwhelming majority of our clients are Native Hawaiians. Mari and I have worked with them, in various capacities, for over 20 years (since my Habitat for Humanity days). I also did a two-year stint as the Office of Hawaiian Affairs' housing department manager. We have also created about 10 Native Hawaiian nonprofits, written about 30 Native Hawaiian business plans, and have taught 10-week Native Hawaiian entrepreneurship workshops.

Success Stories

Honolulu Habitat for Humanity

When I joined Habitat, the affiliate had averaged building three homes a year for the previous 11 years. By 2002, I had won a $10 million RFP proposal to build 45 three-bedroom affordable housing units. We did not have the in-house expertise to build an entire subdivision, so I partnered with a for-profit affordable housing builder. Our joint venture was awarded the contract. I brought in other partners to help fund the homes. As a result, our affiliate only funded six homes. The other 39 were funded by the USDA Rural Development, a local bank, and a local mortgage company.

Why? Because all three entities had programs that helped low-income families buy their own homes. Everybody won!

LESSON: partnerships help.

While at Habitat, the Federal Home Loan Bank of Seattle announced $10M in grants available for affordable housing projects. They funded 50 nonprofit projects with the $10M, and I got $2.3M (23%) of the pot. NPOs that asked for $10,000 got $10,000. Those that asked for $50,000, got $50,000. I asked for $2.3M and got $2.3M.

LESSON: If you ask big, you may get big (IF you justify the ask).

Pearl Harbor Aviation Museum

The museum's secondary mission is to provide Hawaii's youth, ages preschool to high school, STEM (Science, Technology, Engineering, Mathematics) education. Leadership believed that empowering our next Hawaii generation to lead and take on future challenges required vastly improving their math and science competencies and strengthening their life skills (the values and character that guide decision-making). Museum staff used kites and the museum's 52 fixed-wing and rotary-wing aircraft to get visiting youth excited about STEM-based on the science of flight and aerodynamic principles.

When I arrived at the museum, I asked the department heads what items they had been unable to get funding for. One need was bus transportation for disadvantaged public schools that could not afford the $300 bus cost to bring their students to the museum. In 2017, I wrote a proposal to a Chicago foundation requesting $50,000 to provide bus transportation so 5,400 disadvantaged students could visit the museum. Not only was it funded, but in 2018 the foundation sent me an email recommending I apply for *another* $50,000.

I wrote a proposal to help bring 7,200 students to the MathAlive! exhibit (detailed below), and that proposal was also funded!

LESSON: ASK for what you need.

MathAlive!

Many of Hawaii's youth often find limited education and career options. Sixty-five percent of Hawaii's 284 public schools are Title I schools. Therefore, they have large concentrations of low-income students. These institutions so overwhelmed in merely providing basic classroom tasks are often unprepared to address combined skills instruction. They look to informal educational partners to supply the increasing need for advanced learning.

To help get Hawaii's youth interested in STEM, the museum's management researched bringing the MathAlive! international traveling exhibit to Hawaii. MathAlive! is an interactive and inspiring exhibition exploring the world of mathematics. It was designed by Raytheon and NASA and featured hands-on STEM training models and challenges.

Designed for families and students, the exhibition excites students by making real-world connections between math and the activities students already love to do--video games, sports, fashion, music, robotics, and more. It enables students and teachers to explore exciting STEM-powered activities such as designing video games, engineering cities of the future, and riding snowboards.

At that point, the exhibit had traveled to Phoenix, Houston, Boston, San Diego, Kuwait, Saudi Arabia, Qatar, and Australia. We wanted the exhibit to come to Hawaii, but we were initially advised the exhibit normally went to areas with larger youth communities, meaning Hawaii was just too small. In response, I drafted what I considered a compelling proposal. We proposed installing a free-standing, 4,000-square-foot, air-conditioned building on the museum grounds to house the exhibit. I got the proposal approved by the museum's management and submitted it. To our surprise, the proposal was accepted, and the museum hosted the exhibit from November 2018 to August 2019.

LESSON: If you believe fervently in your project, do not be deterred just because someone says no. If you are reasonably persistent, you may get a yes.

Council for Native Hawaiian Advancement (CNHA)

The mission of CNHA is "to enhance the cultural, economic, political, and community development of Native Hawaiians. We envision a socially and economically sustainable Hawaiian community empowered through self-governance." Since 2001, CNHA has designed initiatives that deliver hundreds of educational workshops and symposiums statewide and throughout the Pacific. After our long history of working with Native Hawaiian organizations, we were thrilled when CNHA became our company's first 12-month grant writing client. Between November 2019 and September 2020, our company wrote proposals that got CNHA $1,975,000 in grants from state, federal, and private foundations.

LESSON: Booker T. Washington (the former slave who became a leading 19th century African American intellectual that founded Tuskegee Normal and Industrial Institute (now Tuskegee University)) advised black people to "drop your bucket where you are." As a black man in Hawaii, I dropped my bucket here and made a place for myself based strictly on merit and "the content of my character."

Proposal Reviewer Experience

One of the best things I did to improve the quality of my grant writing was to serve on city, state, and federal grant proposal review panels. Those experiences allowed me to view the grant proposal evaluation process from the evaluator's perspective. It totally shifted my grant writing paradigm. Up to that point, it had all been about me, the writer. After these experiences, my proposals became about the reviewers. My job is to make it easy for the evaluators to say, "this one should be funded." **LESSON**: Learn the process from the evaluators' point-of-view.

Papi's Grant Writing Theorems

Our company focuses on larger foundations and government (city, state, and federal) grant proposals. I am often asked why we have that particular focus. I think of Willie Sutton, the famous 20s and 30s American banker robber. When he was finally caught, a reporter asked why he robbed banks. He responded by saying, "because that's where the money is." When people ask me why I focus on large federal and foundation grants, I use his analogy and respond, "because that's where the money is."

When I did a drill down on my "things I wish I knew when I started grant writing" list, I came up with:

Theorem #1: In general, established NPOs waste too much time and too much effort seeking small grants.

Theorem #2: The grant writing process is essentially the same for small grants or larger and/or government grants. The NPO still has to justify how it will use every cent.

Theorem #3: NPOs requesting larger amounts get more respect from stakeholders AND funders.

Theorem #4: When NPOs request larger amounts, even if they are not fully funded, they may still get more funds than they had originally thought possible.

Theorem #5: In grant writing, like in sports, if you don't shoot, you don't score. So, you just keep on shooting because some of those bad boys will go in "nothin' but net!"

Theorem #6: Short sentences and short paragraphs are easier for evaluators to process mentally.

Theorem #7: Spelling and grammar DO count!

Theorem #8: Before submitting your proposal, have an objective person read it.

Theorem #9: Ensure your budget aligns with your narrative.

Theorem #10: Follow ALL application instructions.

Theorem #11: Do a good job EVERY time!

Theorem #12: Develop/maintain a reputation for being fair, honest, dedicated, ethical, and of unquestioned integrity.

Unexpected Consequence

A truly satisfying aspect of my grant writing career is driving around our island and seeing the results of projects and dreams I helped fulfill -e.g., an affordable housing subdivision, a control tower elevator's renovation, thousands of Hawaii's youth visiting the aviation museum, entrepreneurs launching businesses, etc. I have come to appreciate that unanticipated internal pride over time. I tell my clients that "you got boots on the ground and are doing the heavy lifting. I do not have your expertise and cannot do what you do. But I can create a compelling, competitive, and fundable proposal that will get you the money you need to do what you do!"

Jennifer Yarbrough

Website: www.jdyarbrough.com
Email: jen@jenthegrantguru.com
Facebook: Jennifer Yarbrough
Facebook Group: Nonprofit Leaders Impacting Lives
IG: Jen The Grant Guru
LinkedIn: Jennifer Yarbrough

Jennifer Yarbrough has spent over 30 years working in the areas of grant writing, major fundraising, strategic planning, program development, and organizational assessment for some of the largest nonprofit organizations in the country.

Jennifer has trained thousands of nonprofit executives, board members, and fundraising staff, both nationally and internationally, and has raised over $400 million in funding throughout her career. She has developed introductory and advanced trainings to support brand new nonprofits, starting with a sustainability plan to follow. Her work as a trainer and coach has afforded her many platforms to speak at conferences, radio, and organizational retreats. Jennifer is affectionately referred to as "The Grant Guru" and "The Nonprofit Guru."

A graduate of Tuskegee University, Jennifer received a Bachelor of Science in Political Science. She began her career writing her first grant proposal as a class assignment in college. The grant was awarded $250,000 from HUD for Drug & Alcohol elimination in the public housing community of Kingsport, TN.

From there, she has grown to hold every single job in a nonprofit and expertly shows leaders how program, finance, and fund development must work together for organizational sustainability.

Currently, Jennifer is the Pastor of Good Ground Christian Assembly and works full time as a consultant, master coach, trainer, and public speaker. She likes to say that Paul built tents to support him in ministry, and she builds nonprofits. She provides coaching to board members, nonprofit leaders, fundraisers, and entrepreneurs. Jennifer can be reached at jen@jenthegrantguru.com or www.jdyarbrough.com.

THE MONEY MATTERS OF GETTING GRANT FUNDING

Money. The hottest topic for all non-profit organizations, both big and small. There is this ongoing struggle between the notion that it is a 'pain in the neck' and 'necessary evil' by most. When speaking to leaders about their need to plan for funding and strategic systems, it is seen as an inconvenience and an annoying task.

The bottom line is this, regardless of the dominant attitude towards money in your non-profit, the irrefutable truth is that non-profit's need money to survive. All organizations do. There is a huge false perception that starting an organization with "passion" alone is enough to start, scale, and sustain a program. It's also false that an "idea" driven by the desire to "help others" will spark momentum and engagement from communities, funders, and other money sources.

It is interesting how many leaders say, "I didn't start my non-profit to make any money,"...but it always turns to money when they end up having to pay for everything out of their own pockets. I would argue that the leaders who start their non-profit businesses without a clear plan to start, scale, and sustain their business are, in fact, "fearful leaders." Why do I say this?

Most leaders that I speak to do not write out their plans for the program because they:

- Fear they will do it wrong or make a mistake

- Fear their dream is too big

- Fear that they will not get the support they really hope for and need

- Fear of rejection by funders and potential donors

- Fear the people closest to them will not support them

- Fear to invest in expert knowledge because they are not confident it will really benefit them or their organization

- Fear sharing their programs with others because someone may "take their idea"

- Fear that they will be "judged" for being brand new

- Fear of delegating or asking for help

- Fear of asking for money or bothering people

- Fear that they sound like they are "begging" when asking for money

- Fear of "bothering" donors or making them angry

This is where I want you to pause for a moment. Let's just think about the complex problem that occurs when a person decides to start a business but then give all of their goods away. Did you catch that? A business has started, and there is no plan or process to generate income. It is **IMPOSSIBLE** to sustain any business with no money coming in to support all that it entails to run programs and operations every single day.

In the non-profit sector, like in every business sector, leadership is key to business strength and sustainability. Statistics show that 83% of non-profit's do not grow or scale. A vast majority of organizations remain small for three reasons--and money is not one of them. The three reasons are:

1. Organizations do not have a strategic plan

2. Organizations are not able to articulate impact

3. Lack of strong leadership, clear vision, and goal setting to direct and grow the organization

Founder's Syndrome

Not to "pigeonhole" or cast everyone in the same light, but there is a large number of organizations that could be classified as suffering from Founder's Syndrome. Founder's Syndrome (also founderitis) is the difficulty faced by organizations where one or more founders maintain disproportionate influence and control following the establishment of the organization, leading to a wide range of problems.

The founder driven purely by passion but lacks the creativity and capacity to grow the organization becomes the factor that limits (and ultimately destroys) the organization's potential. To be clear, the syndrome occurs in both nonprofit and for-profit businesses. For most nonprofit organizations, this type of leadership condition drastically limits the program's growth and success. It may cause division among the board and other volunteers as the scale of demands on the organization increases. It may result in outright failure.

While there are many common characteristics of this type of leader, the following are directly related to funding potential:

- The founder is "the decider." All important decisions come from him or her, with little input from others.

- Members of the board of directors and staff are recruited by the founder and act primarily out of their loyalty to this person rather than the organization. Instead of governing, the board merely rubber stamps founder suggestions.

- The organization lacks a clear succession plan.

These conditions leave organizations in a vulnerable position. Among other risks, if something should happen to the founder, how would the organization carry on?

It's worth noting that founders' reluctance to loosen their grip isn't necessarily due to a power-hungry need to control. Founders may fear that the organization would falter without their continued connection — for example, donations might drop off if the founder isn't associated with the organization anymore. Or founders might have invested so much of themselves and their lives in the organization that they simply can't imagine a different path.

What tends to be the driving motivation to start the nonprofit is:

- "I want to start a new nonprofit, so I can qualify for grants!"

- "I can't do this on my own and need board members and staff to help me run things"

- "I have been doing this for free and could get paid for my work if I become the Director of my own organization."

- "I am passionate about my cause and want to dedicate my life to this "mission."

Again, with what was just shared, we have to remember that every business must have money coming in to survive. We all know that money doesn't grow on trees. If it did, starting a nonprofit would be as easy as planting a money tree. In a world where money doesn't come quite so easily, starting a nonprofit with no cash, or plan to raise any, can be a challenge. Luckily, the task isn't impossible. Since you are reading this book, you are learning the steps that will help you determine your nonprofit's needs and solutions to finding the grant money necessary to achieve your mission.

For many nonprofits, and the reason that so many do not get grant funding, the process of "getting a grant" or "writing a grant proposal" is a mystery, like an old family recipe with secret ingredients.

For over 30 years, I have been helping people de-mystify this process and to understand that, like a recipe, creating a compelling proposal simply requires common ingredients put together in a logical and understandable sequence using tried and true techniques.

Before we move forward, let's talk about what a grant is and is not. In most cases, a grant is support that does not need to be repaid. Usually, it is in the form of money, but it may be technical assistance or training. Grants are usually awarded after the submission of a written proposal. So, the "grant" is the funding or other assistance received as a result of a grant proposal (also referred to as an application). A grant is not the written document that we submit to a potential funding source!

Each funder sets its own eligibility criteria for grant applicants, and eligible applicants are typically nonprofit organizations or public agencies. Nonprofits are often required to be 501(c)(3) organization under the IRS. Here's a link to IRS information on nonprofits: Exemption Requirements – 501(c)(3) Organizations. Grants to for-profit entities or to private individuals do exist; however, they are far less common.

Each funder will also have its own application process, and the degree of detail required will vary. Here, we'll talk about the basic recipe for a grant proposal, understanding that some funders may require extra and/or different information—special ingredients.

Let's take a look at the basic ingredients required in a typical proposal and how to include them.

1) **Proof that your organization is strong and viable** – Funders look carefully at the applicant organization's history, leadership, and track record. You have the opportunity to offer clear and compelling descriptions of your organization's accomplishments and program impact (including statistics and examples is always helpful). The potential funder views the highlight of your achievements as essential and meaningful. If your organization is new and its track record is brief or just starting, look to your knowledge of the "need" or program your organization is solving. Your ability to describe how you will bring about change (this will provide credibility) and stress community partnerships will build the funder's confidence in the new organization's ability to achieve results. Consider this section of the proposal as a resume for your

organization – your goal is to impress the reader with the organization's credibility and qualifications.

2) **Compelling description of what "success" will look like after your organization addresses the situation** – This section of a grant proposal is typically called **the problem statement, statement of need, or something similar.** Your discussion of the problem to be addressed lays the foundation for the program plan, and if this section is weak, so is the rest of the proposal. A strong statement of the problem will address the following:

- **Who is affected?** What are their qualities or characteristics? How many people are affected, and what are the causes/reasons that they are in the place of needing help? This context about the problem is what drives the funder's interest and creates a case of urgency. Your understanding of the target population is critical. There's a story to tell, and it's your job to tell it.
- **Why is the problem significant?** Why should the funder care about what's happening? There are urgent and compelling

problems all around us. What is at stake if your program does not go forth? If there is credible research on the subject, discuss it. It can sometimes be useful to show how the local problem your program is solving compares with the state or national situation.

- **Why is the problem occurring?** Identifying the causes of the "problem" or situation(s) addressed will lead you directly to possible solutions. Remember, your program is a set of "strategic" activities designed to solve the problem--and bring about change. Your program participants know exactly why their problem exists. It is very important that you speak to them and assess if they are ready to do the problem-solving work. Their responses are invaluable and can help challenge preconceived notions that you, your team, or even a potential funding partner might have about the situation. Avoid assumptions.

One final note: the situation for which your organization is seeking a grant should generally not be about your own organization. Rather, it should be about those you are proposing to serve.

3. **A clear statement of expected change and what the people will look like when they leave your program** – After you have clearly laid the plan for lasting change, it's time to specify the outcomes (impact and lasting change) the grant-funded program will achieve. Funders use lots of different terms and may call these program outcomes, objectives, or even goals. Whatever they are called, think about this: what do you expect to result from the program your organization will run? **Propose outcomes that are specific, measurable**, and that will be accomplished within a set time frame. If you have defined the problem well, the outcomes logically and systematically follow.

4. **Well-thought-out plan of action** – Next, lay out how your organization will accomplish the projected outcomes. **Funders may call this section methods, approach, plan of action, program plan, or something else.** No matter what they call it, this is what your organization plans to do when it gets the grant. Include who, what, when, where, and how. Explain it like you would explain a program to someone who knew nothing about it.

WHO – Who will be in charge of getting the work done? What are their qualifications? Who will be served or impacted? How many people will be served each year? Are there any specific criteria for the people in the program? Discuss any collaborative efforts with other agencies or organizations that will be part of the program.

WHAT – What will be happening? What are the specific strategies that will be used? How long will the solution take? What goals will be achieved? What resources will be used to get the job done?

WHEN – What is the timeline for activities? It's helpful to lay out a graphic timeline with three columns that describe who, what they'll do, and when.

WHERE – Where will the work take place? Where will you find program participants? Where will the program participants go when they leave your program?

HOW – How will the work be accomplished? How long with the program be?

Finally, one more question to answer – **Why this approach?** Have others used this approach and been successful? Is this approach considered to be a best practice or a model in your field? Share your rationale. It adds credibility to your proposal if you can demonstrate that you have a broad understanding of what other organizations in your field are doing and have learned.

Plan to evaluate – Nearly every funder will ask for a description of how you will evaluate the grant-funded program. Funders want to know that their investment in your organization was a good one. Simply put, the evaluation plan describes how your organization: **(1) will measure the level to which the program is achieving the expected outcomes; and 2) will document that program activities are accomplishing the planned results, as well as any course corrections you're making and why.**

The outcomes are what the funder is interested in. They are giving money for the results that your program will accomplish. When you are mapping out your program plan of success and outcomes, ask yourself these questions:

1. How will you know when you have accomplished them?

2. What benchmarks are you expecting to see, and what are the indicators that will show the program is headed in the right direction? Describe those benchmarks and what they will tell you about results. Describe what data will be collected and analyzed, and by whom. Then, describe what you will do with what you are learning. Will you be able to use those results to help guide future program development? If so, describe how that will be done. Remember that **outcomes are all about results**, so how will you monitor results? This is what many funders call the "outcome evaluation" plan.

Then, think about how your organization can improve the program from day one. How will the organization know whether the program approach is working or when revisions to the plan are warranted? Typically, some of the things that may be monitored are client participation; community support; feedback from clients, collaborators, or others; client satisfaction; and feedback from others (i.e., parents, teachers, etc.). Analysis of the situation can help you modify the approach so that it's more effective. This part of the evaluation plan is often called **"process evaluation."**

Plan for sustaining the program – Grants are great and a huge financial benefit for the organization (usually), but they are not designed to fund the entire program or operational expenses on an on-going basis. They are generally short-lived. When you are applying for grants, you must have a plan for the program after the grant ends. If this is a program or service that continues, it is important that you strategize ideas for ongoing funding (aside from seeking more grants!). Think about potential multiple funding mechanisms that can be explored for **long-term sustainability.** Perhaps your organization excels at community fundraising. Maybe there is potential for contracts with government or for-profit corporations who need your service. A product or service might be something to explore.

In this section, also describe who else will be supporting the program. Support from other sources, whether cash or in-kind, may provide leverage for the grant. Don't forget about what your own organization will contribute, like office space, administrative support, or whatever you are able to provide.

Realistic budget – Now, it's time to talk about the money to achieve the plan. Be clear about how much the program will cost. Be specific and account for all the ingredients in your program recipe.

Get a piece of paper, and let's walk through it right now. Start by making a chart with four columns:

Column 1 – Line Items: Use your organization's chart of accounts to list the line items that must be addressed in budgeting for the grant-funded program.

Chart of Accounts: The chart of accounts (or COA) is a numbered list that categorizes your financial activity into different accounts and subaccounts. If you do not have a bookkeeper or account, you should pay very close attention to this section because here is where the expenses and review become crystal clear. Every nonprofit organization has a unique COA that depends on your specific programs, revenue sources, and activities. In general, your COA should follow some standard guidelines and numbering format.

A chart of accounts is commonly numbered as follows:

Statement of Financial Position

Assets: 1000-1999

Liabilities: 2000-2999

Equity/Net Assets: 3000-3999

Statement of Activities

Revenue: 4000-4999

Expenses: 5000+

This means that any assets owned by your nonprofit (like bank accounts, investments, property, and equipment) should be numbered in the 1000 range. Liabilities (like loans, mortgages, and accounts payable) should be in the 2000 range. Your organization's restricted and unrestricted net assets should be numbered in the 3000 range. Revenue from donations or sales should be in the 4000 range, and expenses for programs, utilities, salaries, and everything else should be numbered as 5000 or above.

When you're numbering your accounts, follow these three rules:

1. **Keep things simple.** You don't need separate accounts for paper, pens, envelopes, and staples; you can just have one account for office supplies.

2. **Group similar accounts together.** It's easier to read and understand your financial reports when your accounts are listed in a logical order.

3. **Leave room for growth.** You can't group similar accounts together if all the numbers are already taken! Think about how your needs might change in the future and leave gaps between your account numbers so you can add new accounts later.

Below is a sample chart of accounts for nonprofit organizations. A nonprofit chart of accounts for your organization is the list of each account that money comes into, or out of, in your organization. The word *chart* just makes it sound fancy. This list is created by your organization and will vary depending on your nonprofit's needs. Your organization will only have one chart of accounts, so make sure to create one that makes sense for your operations.

Examples of A Chart of Accounts

When accounts are created in your accounting system, they are organized using names and numbers. For the most part, account numbers are up to you and how you would like to organize them. However, the standard number ranges applied to each account is as followed:

1010: Checking (Bank Account)

1030: Savings (Bank Account)

1210: Accounts Receivable

1310: Inventory

1410: Prepaid Expenses

1510: Equipment

2010: Accounts Payable

2100: Accrued Salaries

2110: Accrued Payroll Taxes

2115: Accrued Employee Benefits

2150: Accrued Property Taxes

2200: Credit Card Payable

3100: Unrestricted Net Assets

4010: Donations and Grants – Individuals

4020: Donations and Grants – Government

4030: Donations and Grants – Foundations

4110: Special Events – Sponsorships

4120: Special Events – Auction

4130: Special Events – Ticket Sales

4200: Program Revenue

4300: Sales of Merchandise

4500: Membership Dues

4600: In-Kind Contributions

4700: Temporarily Restricted Income

4800: Permanently Restricted Income

4900: Interest Income

4910: Dividend Income

5000: Salaries and Wages

5010: Payroll Taxes

5030: Health Insurance

6000: Fundraising Expenses

6100: Special Event Expenses

6200: Program Expenses

6300: Marketing and Branding

6310: Advertising

6410: Contract Services

6420: Accounting Services

6430: Legal Services

6510: Rent Expense

6520: Utilities

6525: Telecommunications

6530: Maintenance and Repairs

6540: Office Supplies

6550: Printing and Copying

6560: Postage and Shipping

6570: Licenses and Permits

6610: Bank Fees

6620: Merchant Service Fees

6810: Board Expenses

6820: Miscellaneous Expenses

Remember, this is only an example – your nonprofit might have different types of revenue and expenses or own different assets that will alter your chart of accounts.

Column 2 – Total Program Budget: This column shows the cost of everything that will go into the program, even if it's already covered by other sources.

I will use the example of an after-school center that provides tutoring and homework assistance for low-income children. Once you start the program, you decide to add tutors, art classes, and a sports program. When you are assessing the budgetary needs, think about it this way:

> A _program coordinator_ trains and recruits _the tutors_ and _purchases books, notebooks, and school supplies_. The art program requires an _artist's time, supplies, space for artmaking, and access to paint and paint cleaner._

To offer a sports program, your organization <u>rents</u> the nearby gym, <u>hires four coaches, employs a volunteer coordinator to recruit parents and other assistant coaches, and purchases equipment.</u>

The specific costs of a program — books, art supplies, coaches — are called *direct* costs. Keep in mind that each of the three programs also depends on materials and services provided by the people who work on behalf of the entire organization, such as the full-time executive director, the part-time administrative assistant, and the bookkeeper. Each of the three after-school programs also uses the organization's offices, utilities, telephones, and printed materials. The costs that the various programs share — such as the executive director's salary, admin's times, bookkeeping services, rent, and telephone bills — are *indirect* costs. You can think of these shared costs as the glue that holds the nonprofit together.

Direct costs are pretty straightforward. For example, you know what you have to pay your tutors per hour how many hours they work. However, indirect costs can be more unclear, and not because they're the organizational glue. They can be unclear if you are not sure how to divide them accurately with all of the other organizational activities.

Let me step off the grant budget path for just a moment. You must know how much your program costs in order to successfully get grant funding. The budget that you present to the prospective funder is a tool that they use to evaluate the strength of your "business" model to invest in. 90% of grant funding is not denied because of the program--they are denied because the organization does not have a budget. Just imagine what the funder is thinking when an organization can't explain how they spend their money. It makes them wonder how you will spend the money you are asking them to give you.

Column 3 - Other Funding: For each line item, show funding and the value of other resources that will become from sources other than the requested grant. Be sure to include what your own organization will provide. The amounts in this column are sometimes called "matching resources," "leveraged funds," or "cost-sharing."

Column 4 – **Amount of The Requested Grant:** The difference between Column 2 and Column 3 is your requested grant amount. It is important to also note that, typically, grant proposals include budgets for one-year time periods. If you are submitting a multi-year request, calculate each year separately and include a summary that shows the multi-year total.

Also, remember the budget is a projection of what will come. The budget is a forward-thinking process. Therefore, you want to think not just about what the line items would cost today, but what they will cost when you actually incur the expense. Will salaries go up? Will the program grow or expand to include more people? Will you have to hire more people to work in the program?

The in-kind donations should be calculated in the total program budget and then indicated in the other funding column. The in-kind value should be based on what you would actually pay in your community for that item if you had to pay cash for it.

Be certain that there are no expenses in your budget request that are unexplained. Some funding sources will ask for a budget narrative, which gives you an opportunity to explain each item, how you calculated it, and how it is important to your proposed program. Now, you get to show off your math skills.

Summary

Once you've completed the budget, you've completed the body of the proposal - the main entree! Now, you're ready to write a summary.

A summary is brief and may be just a few sentences, but it gives an overview of the entire proposal. While it is written last, it is almost always placed at the very beginning of a grant proposal.

Since it is usually the first thing that reviewers will see, create it with care! Pick out a key point from every section of the narrative and write a sentence about it. Then, summarize the budget and how much you are requesting. That's it...all done!

Attachments

Sometimes funders require that you send additional attachments along with your proposal. Typically, requested items include brief resumes of key staff, job descriptions, letters of support or commitment from collaborating organizations, your organization's current operating budget, and a copy of your organization's 501(c)(3) letter from the Internal Revenue Service. Have these typical attachments on hand and keep them up to date so they're ready to go when you need them.

Grant Budget Examples

Personnel Detail

Personnel Budget

Executive Director (10%)	$8,000
Program Director (30%)	$19,000
Program Coordinator (75%)	$30,000
Program Assistants (2 @ 50%)	$40,000
Subtotal	**$97,000**
Fringe Benefits (@ 20%)	$19,400
Total Salaried Personnel	$116,400
Part-time Instructors (3)	$60,000

Evaluator	$40,000
Total Consultants	$100,00
TOTAL PERSONNEL	**$216,400**

***** Percentages reflect the time worked on the project.

Direct Expenses

Rent	$72,000
Utilities	$1,700
Insurance	$4,500
Business fee and services	$5,500
Postage	$2,250
Printing	$7,000
Internet service and phone	$1,140
Equipment rental	$900
Supplies	$4,000

Travel	$1,430
Entertaining	$2,500
Professional development	$3,000
Conference fees, memberships, subs.	$1,800
Other expenses	$1,050
Depreciation	$2,100
Total non-personnel	$110,870
TOTAL EXPENSES	$673,580

*****Note that similar expenses (rent and utilities, professional

development, conference fees) are grouped together.

Indirect Expenses

Administrative + Fundraising expenses = Indirect expenses (AKA overhead)

Indirect expenses / Total expenses = indirect rate

Income in a grant request budget

Requested from the Johnson Foundation	$10,000
Southwest Airlines (in-kind committed)	$2,500
Smith Family Foundation (received)	$10,000
Community Foundation (pending)	$15,000
Participant fees	$5,000
TOTAL	$47,500

*****Note that the requested amount appears first and is clearly labeled as such.

Income formatting

Government	$400,000
Foundation	$190,000
Corporations	$140,000
Individuals	$30,000
Subtotal Contributed Income	**$760,000**
Earned Income	
Sports League Fees	$25,000
Interest and investment	$85,000
Subtotal Earned Income	**$110,000**
Total Income	**$870,000**

Government	$400,000
Federal grants	$370,000
State grants	$30,00
Subtotals Grants	$400,000
Foundation	$190,000
Corporations	$140,000
Individuals	$30,000
Subtotal Contributed Income	**$760,000**
Earned Income	
Sports League Fees	$25,000
Interest and investment	$85,000
Subtotal Earned Income	**$110,000**
Total Income	**$870,000**

*****The second example breaks down the government grants, showing the heavy reliance on federal grants; this might or might not be a positive for your application (depending on whether it had been obtained at the time of this foundation request).

Operating Budget

Expenses

Executive Director	$60,000
Administrative personnel (3)	$195,000
Artistic personnel (2)	$120,000
Support personnel (3.5)	$108,000
Fringe benefits and payroll taxes @ 17%	$61,710
Total Personnel	$544,710
Rent	$72,000
Utilities	$1,700
Insurance	$4,500
Business fees and services	$5,500
Postage	$2,250

Printing	$7,000
Internet service and phone	$1,140
Equipment rental	$900
Supplies	$4,000
Travel	$1,430
Entertaining	$2,500
Professional development	$3,000
Conference fees, memberships, subs.	$1,800
Other expenses	$1,050
Depreciation	$2,100
Total non-personnel	**$110,870**
Total Expenses	**$655,580**

Income

Admissions	$8,300
Service fees	$3,000
Interest income	$550
Total earned income	**$11,850**
Individuals	$192,150
Fundraising events (net)	$9,000
Foundations	$220,000
Corporations	$19,000
Local government	$185,000
Other government	$16,000
Total contributed income	**$642,050**

Total Income	$655,900
Surplus (deficit)	$320

Multi-Year Budget

Sports Program

EXPENSES

Personnel	Year 1	Year 2	Total	Six-Month Interim Report Actuals
Coaches (3 @ 20%)	27,000	27,000	54,000	13,548
Referees @ 5%	3,500	3,500	7,000	1,600
Program Coordinator @ 5%	3,000	3,000	6,000	$1,500
Fringe benefits @ 19%	6,365	6,365	12,730	3,163
Subtotal salaried personnel	39,865	39,865	79,730	19,811
Intern Stipends (3)	66,000	66,000	132,000	33,000

	105,865	105,865	211,730	52,811
Program Expenses				
Marketing/outreach	5,000	500	5,500	4,921
Supplies	600	1,000	1,600	302
Travel	1,000	2,000	3,000	98
Photocopying	800	1,900	2,700	110
Telephone	100	400	500	30
Postage/Delivery	400	400	800	338
Finals/Playoff games expenses	20,000	20,000	40,000	8,000
Contingency	300	1,200	1,500	15
Subtotal direct expenses	28,200	28,200	56,400	5,517

Indirect costs @ 15%	17,160	23,010	40,170	8,794
Total Expenses	151,225	157,075	308,300	67,500
INCOME				
Rotary Club	75,000	75,000	150,000	75,000
Wells Fargo	50,000	50,000	100,000	50,000
Community Trust	10,000	10,000	20,000	10,000
Citizens Trust	8,000	12,000	20,000	8,000
Shelton Family Foundation	7,500	0	7,500	7,500
Douglas Family Trust (Pending)	0	10,000	10,000	0

TOTAL INCOME	150,500	157,000	307,500	150,500
Surplus (Deficit)	19,275	-19,275	0	83,081

Financial Review

While an application may be completed well and the program is strong, your budget also needs to be well-documented and reflect the requirements of the grant program. The funders conduct a cost analysis, reviewing each line item and the overall proposed budget to ensure compliance with statutory and financial regulations. Additionally, the financial review also factors in the total budget for the grant program in relation to how much money each application requests.

As a hint, see if you can answer the following questions:

1. Which payroll employee will spend the most time on this project?

2. Where will the project take place?

3. How many activities will there be?

4. What will these activities consist of?

5. How will it be paid for?

When you submit a grant proposal, in most cases, the proposal will be evaluated by a panel of reviewers convened by the funder (i.e., the private foundation or government agency that posted the opportunity). To make the process as fair and objective as possible, those evaluating the proposal rate it against a set of predetermined criteria. Sometimes the evaluation criteria and how they are weighted even appear in the solicitation itself, providing applicants with valuable information about how to structure their proposal.

The proposal reviewers face the daunting task of reading and scoring a mountain of proposals to get the pile down to a reasonable number, and from this short-listed group, down to the ultimate winner (or winners, if the funding budget provides for multiple awards). As you can imagine, slogging through a pile of grant proposals is not a fun task. To reduce the number of proposals to be reviewed, funders look for reasons to eliminate proposals from consideration. As a grant reviewer, I can attest that what trips an applicant up often is the failure to follow directions regarding the required formatting of a proposal. Other times, the issues can be more serious, such as failing to follow the proposal guidelines regarding required content (including submitting the required budget content).

Conclusion

In conclusion, do not be intimidated by the grant writing process. In fact, go after as many as you can. Grants represent 17-20% of your overall budget. This is close to $4 trillion that goes to the non-profit industry every year. You absolutely should be getting your share of those funds.

As you approach the grant writing process, here are some general tips that should help you through it:

- Begin early

- Apply early and often

- Answer all questions

- If rejected, revise your proposal and apply again.

- Give them what they want.

- Follow the application guidelines exactly

- Be specific

- Be realistic in designing the project

Trust the process and remember that activity is not impact. Your organization is providing a valuable service and serving real people and programs in the community. You are not begging for money; you are an asset to the community. At least 1,000 people are praying for a solution to their problems, and your non-profit is that solution. Never ever forget that **YOUR MISSION MATTERS.**

Most new and small nonprofits, with operating budgets of less than $500,000, spend roughly $3,000 each year on training, conferences, and software, hoping to raise more money. Not only do 77% miss their budgeted revenue goals, but they are also actually raising less money than the previous year. This means that even with the resources invested, most organizations are actually losing ground – and frantically turn to foundations and their donors to make up the difference.

Every funder wants to see its grantees succeed. Foundations and donors hope their grantees raise enough revenue to create impact and sustain their programs. The inclination is to find a way to help. However, in the final analysis, funding to bring on a development director, hire a consultant, or attend a conference too often falls short of the transformation envisioned. We must do better.